Perfect Daughters

Adult Daughters Of Alcoholics

To Scottie,
best wishes & dreams

Robert J. Ackerman

5/14/93

Robert J. Ackerman

Health Communications, Inc.
Deerfield Beach, Florida

Robert J. Ackerman, Ph.D.
Indiana, Pennsylvania

Grateful acknowledgment is made for permission to reprint excerpts from the following works: ALL I REALLY NEED TO KNOW I LEARNED IN KINDERGARTEN by Robert Fulghum, by permission of Villard Books, a Division of Random House, Inc. Copyright ©1986, 1988 by Robert Fulghum. BORN TO PLEASE: COMPLIANT WOMEN/CONTROLLING MEN by Karen Blaker, Ph.D., by permission of St. Martin's Press, Inc. New York. Copyright ©1988 by Karen Blaker. I AM AN ADULT CHILD OF AN ALCOHOLIC by Thomas Perrin, by permission of Thomas W. Perrin, Inc. Copyright ©1983 by Thomas Perrin.

Library of Congress Cataloging-in-Publication Data

Ackerman, Robert J.
    Perfect daughters: adult daughters of alcoholics / by Robert J. Ackerman.
        p.   cm.
    Bibliography: p.
    ISBN 1-55874-040-6
    1. Adult children of alcoholics — United States.   2. Daughters — United States.   3. Co-dependence (Psychology)   4. Adjustment (Psychology)   I. Title.
    HV5132.A265   1989   89-15247
    362.29'23—dc20   CIP

©1989 Robert J. Ackerman

ISBN 1-55874-040-6

Publisher: Health Communications, Inc.
                3201 S.W. 15th Street
                Deerfield Beach, Florida 33442

Cover design by Reta Thomas

Dedication

To all adult daughters
and especially to
Kimberly, Mary and Debbie

Contents

PART THREE
Save You, Save Me

PART FOUR
Discovery And Recovery Of Me

Acknowledgments

The number of people who have encouraged me and supported me in the writing of this book has been numerous. I thank them all and am especially grateful to the following:

To my research colleague, friend and confidant, Judith A. Michaels, a special thank you. Her support, research skills and ideas helped me all the way from developing the first adult daughter questionnaire to the writing of the final page.

Thank you to Kimberly Roth Ackerman for her willingness to tell me, "Do this over; it needs more work," and her silent, but always present belief in me and this project.

A special thank you to my friend Edward Gondolf for his research skills and help with organizing and analyzing my data on adult daughters.

I wish to thank Linda Sanford and Diane Glynn for their encouragement and support to write this book. Thank you to Marie Stilkind for her editorial assistance.

I appreciate the support of Peter Vegso, Gary Seidler and their staff at Health Communications for their willingness to undertake this project.

I would like to acknowledge the Faculty Research Associate Program of Indiana University of Pennsylvania for supporting my research on adult daughters. I wish to thank Charles Bertness for his computer assistance.

Finally, I am deeply indebted to all of the adult daughters of alcoholics for their willingness to share their emotions, experiences and hopes. Thank you.

The cases and experiences shared throughout this book are real. The names and identities have been changed to insure confidentiality.

Preface

Since the middle of the 1970s I have had the privilege of being involved in one of the most rewarding, emotional and unique experiences that I could imagine. This experience has been my involvement with the children of alcoholics' movement. I have traveled all over this country lecturing, speaking, sharing and listening to children of alcoholics. This is truly a grassroots movement in all respects. It is about children of all ages, who experienced pain in childhood, but want love, joy, health and beauty in their lives. It is a movement about recovery.

As I have participated in this coming together of millions of silent voices, I have observed two things. One is that the children of alcoholics' movement has been swept off its feet by generations of adults who were raised in alcoholic families, adult children if you will, who are now leading the way for the generations behind them. Two, the overwhelming majority of these adult children who are willing to lead and share in order to help others have been women. It is commonly agreed that most children's issues have benefited as a direct result of the Women's Movement in this country. The children of alcoholics' movement is no exception.

During my travels I have listened to many women who shared their stories. It was these stories that made me interested in the subject of adult daughters of alcoholics. Their willingness to express feelings, insights and ways to recovery has opened the door for many who have lived in the isolation and silence of alcoholic families, whether female or male. I am indebted to all of the adult daughters who helped me understand them better, thus enabled me to convey to others what I have learned. If you are an adult daughter of an alcoholic, this book is for you and about you.

Based on research and interviews with women from alcoholic and non-alcoholic families throughout the United States, this book will provide insight and understanding, not only for "adult daughters of alcoholics" themselves, but also for those who love them, live with them, work with them and support them.

More importantly, this book is about recovery. Not all adult daughters are affected the same, nor do all have the same issues, but all of the daughters in this study shared the desire to understand themselves and how to improve their lives. The issues they shared ranged from understanding their personality characteristics and behaviors as adults, relationship and intimacy problems, relating to their parents, their own parenting skills, working through childhood feelings, their addictions, sexuality and a desire for recovery. Perhaps some of these are concerns of yours.

This book is divided into four parts. Part One explores your childhood by exploring how you were raised by an alcoholic parent. Adult daughters expressed very different opinions about having an alcoholic mother as opposed to an alcoholic father. Therefore, much of this section explores the unique relationships and effects that were expressed by daughters of alcoholic mothers and/or alcoholic fathers.

Part Two is on understanding yourself and many of your behaviors. Additionally, we will examine the source of many of your behaviors and how many adult daughters have adapted specific behavior patterns in their lives, both positively and negatively.

Learning to accept your past, your present behaviors and most importantly yourself is the focus of Part Three. Topics in this section include adult daughters' opinions on relationships, parenting, issues with their own parents and working through their own addictions, if any.

Part Four is on discovery and recovery for adult daughters. As you read this book, hopefully you will develop a better understanding of yourself. Am I saying that you do not know who you are now? No, I am asking, "How well do you know yourself?" Do you know why you think and act the way you do, have you reached a decision on the parts of you that you would like to keep, those you would like to discard forever and those that you would like to change? Have you discovered not only your fears, doubts or perceived limitations, but also your many strengths and abilities to improve the quality of your life?

As you read you will see many common themes expressed. However, please keep in mind this theme about all adult children: *I consider all of us to be survivors.*

I am tired of listening and reading books and articles about adult children of alcoholics as if they were the most incredibly dysfunctional adults ever created. I don't know about you, but I have never met an adult child who does not consider herself to be a survivor. Yes, there has been much pain in the lives of children of alcoholics. If you look closely, though, you will see that you have many skills and much more potential. I am writing about the survival, hope, capabilities and strengths that I have witnessed from adult survivors. I am not writing about the despair and hopelessness of victims. The many women in this book overwhelmingly echoed that they are survivors.

The study that this book is based upon was drawn from a national sample of 1209 women in the United States. Of these, 624 were raised in alcoholic families and 585 were raised in non-alcoholic families. In order not to interrupt your reading or your thoughts, all statistics and tables are in the appendix. In addition to the study, 200 women who were raised in alcoholic families were interviewed. Their insights, comments, and personal stories provide the emotional reality about the lives of adult daughters that could never be conveyed from research data alone.

In writing this book, I have faced the greatest of challenges to my skills — myself. I have discovered that I am not "authoring" this book, but rather I am facilitating the words that have been shared. I have called upon my skills as a researcher, writer, counselor, adult child and most importantly, as a listener, to convey to you what I have heard. I hope that I have listened well and that the two goals of this book, a better understanding of adult daughters and providing choices for recovery, will be met. Although these are my goals as a writer, I hope they facilitate your goals as an adult daughter.

Robert J. Ackerman

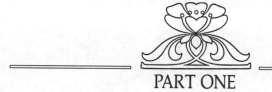

PART ONE

Childhood Revisited

1

Home Groan,
Daughters In Alcoholic Families

Once upon a time in the kingdom of childhood there lived a little girl. She was known as the "princess." Her kingdom was the same as all other kingdoms, she was told, and she wanted to believe this. However, she often found it difficult to understand the royal messages that didn't always make sense. Could there be something wrong with her? Maybe she wasn't like others. Why couldn't she understand what she saw and heard? She wanted to believe that there wasn't anything wrong with her or her kingdom. After all, she was the princess.

"I know," she thought, "I will make it all right and perfect for everyone and then nothing could possibly be wrong." And so the princess spent her childhood making all the things in the kingdom that were wrong appear to be right.

This was not an easy task for her, but she never complained. Besides who could she tell? She was a princess and a protector of the kingdom. When she did ask questions of members of the royal family, she was told "What are you talking about?" or "Don't worry about those things. Little girls are supposed to be happy." Well if that was what little girls were supposed to do, then she would do it. She would show everyone that she could do it better than anyone else and be the best little princess ever. But still the royal messages were unclear and did not go away, especially the ones that she received from her parents, the King and the Queen.

You see, the King and the Queen did not get along very well. Outside of the castle and in the presence of the loyal subjects they pretended that they were the best royal couple in the kingdom. The King, however, was not always so perfect. In fact much of his behavior confused the princess because he was a confusing King. Some days everyone in the kingdom loved him and some days, especially when he drank wine, everyone hid from him. He even treated the princess differently sometimes. On one hand he told her he loved her and on the other, he frightened her.

"Oh well," she thought, "I guess that is what kings do." Besides no one else said anything about the King. He was more like an emperor and no one wanted to tell him about his new clothes.

"I know," thought the little girl, "I will tell the Queen. Surely she will understand and help me." But alas the Queen could not see things clearly either. She had learned to pretend too. After all, she was once a princess herself. The only things that she told the princess were, "Life in the kingdom is hard. Don't say anything to the King or his subjects about drinking wine, and besides, you will find a prince who will take you away from all of this."

Now more confused than ever the princess had another insight to help her understand her childhood kingdom. She decided that the real reason that things appeared different, but really weren't, was because she lived in a magical kingdom.

"That's it," she thought. "This is an illusion. This isn't really happening, and if it isn't really happening, it will go away. What will go away? You know, the things that aren't really here."

Soon the princess began to feel better. Why? Because she began to think like everyone else in the kingdom. Now she got along better, even with the Queen. She learned the magical game and became part of the inner "co-dependent kingdom."

However, she was smarter than other people in the kingdom, but couldn't allow others to know what she knew. And so, she became very good at the magic game and kept her feelings buried in a secret place. Oh, it was such a good hiding place. In fact, it was so secret that soon even she forgot where she had put them.

The years in the kingdom passed and she became an expert in her royal role of "perfect princess." Mixed royal decrees were still everywhere, but she kept them in her heart, always wondering what they really meant and who she really was.

What happened to the little girl in the kingdom? She became a woman.

Donna

I wasn't allowed to cry when I was a little girl. That was noise my dad didn't want to hear. He'd tell you to swallow it or he'd give you something to cry about. Well I feared him so I would fight back the tears. I wouldn't allow myself to be afraid as a child and would turn it into something else. I would go in my room and make believe, pretending that I was a princess living in a castle and everything was okay. Now, when I look back on what my childhood was like, I feel the fears, I feel sadness, I feel hurt and I feel anger.

Growing up in a dysfunctional family where both of my parents were alcoholics, the screaming, yelling, fighting and arguing seemed to me to be normal. That's what normal was to me. It was easy to deny that there were any problems because I lived in a fantasy illusion that this happened in everybody's house. That way I could survive it.

You know, I'd go to a girlfriend's house and I'd see differences from the way things were in my house. I'd leave and say, "Oh, things are the same way at my house, they just don't do that when people are there."

My mother used to drink and I'd come home from school and she'd be passed out. To me, she was napping and that's how I denied that my mother was an alcoholic. Or if I came in and she was drinking and I had brought a friend home, we'd make a joke about it. I'd say it's cocktail hour and it's okay. It took years to accept the fact that my mother was an alcoholic.

I never knew how much it had affected my own life, or even if it had affected my life. When my mother told us that her drinking didn't bother anyone, I believed that. It wasn't until a few months ago when I couldn't explain the depressions that I'd been going through for the past six years, or when I couldn't make my therapy sessions because I just didn't have the will to go that I knew that something was deeply wrong with me. When I couldn't be consistent in my work and with the things that I wanted to do with my children, I knew I had a problem. And when I woke up one morning and I just wanted to die inside, and death was easier than the pain, then I went for help.

Do either of these stories remind you of yourself? If so, you may be one of millions of women who were raised in an alcoholic or other type of dysfunctional family. Although you may feel unique or isolated about your childhood experiences, you are not alone. In fact, there are more than 22 million adults in our country who were raised by one or two alcoholic parents.

For those of you who are aware of the recent children of alcoholics' movement in the United States, you know that children of alcoholics who are now adults are referred to as "adult children of alcoholics" or "adult children" for short. Women who were raised in alcoholic families are referred to as "adult daughters" and they are the focus of this book. If you are unfamiliar with the names or the movement but have lived the experience of having an alcoholic parent, welcome.

The adult children's movement is concerned with two things: growth and recovery. Growth is dependent upon understanding, accepting and working through the experiences of your childhood. Recovery is a process that will allow you to go beyond your childhood experiences and become the type of adult you would like to be. Although you may have had a negative childhood, you can recover and have a healthy positive adulthood.

Can you identify with the many adult children who have become part of this movement?

- Do you want to belong? Do you need to belong?
- Are you the type of adult daughter who has many unresolved issues from your childhood?
- Do you feel that something is missing in your life, but don't know what it is?
- Are you incredibly competent in some aspects of your life, but fear vulnerability in other areas?

Your answers depend upon your childhood, how significantly you were affected, how you cope today as an adult, how well you understand yourself and your desire for recovery.

All of these questions and answers can sound overwhelming, particularly if you believe that your childhood is over and therefore no longer affects you. Or do you recognize that you have problems today but are not sure of the source? After all, are you really different from other women or other adult daughters? Do you feel isolated and unique? It is possible that the source of these answers and your feelings can be found in your childhood. Additionally, many of the things that you think, feel and do today may have their origins in your childhood.

Family: Your Museum Of Memories

In my childhood I was not allowed to express anger. I was only allowed to express happiness and joy. That was acceptable. Anger, sadness and frustration were not acceptable and the only way that I could be accepted by my parents was to

be perfect, to look perfect, to act perfect, to be happy and to
be the model child.

Jill

What was it like to be a child in your family?

For some adult daughters the memories are very vivid.
They can remember many events as if they are happening
today. I often hear others say that they cannot remember
much and have blocked out many of their childhood memories. Still others begin to remember the episodes and
emotions of their childhoods as they begin to talk about
them more.

Many of the adult daughters who said they did not
remember much were concerned that something was
wrong with them because they could not remember. It is
normal for many people to block out unpleasant memories
in their lives. If you do not remember all of your childhood
or cannot recall everything don't worry. After all, you
don't have to have a perfect memory too!

As you recall your alcoholic family, I am sure that you
will experience mixed feelings. This is appropriate since
most alcoholic families are dominated by mixed messages
to their children, such as, "I love you, go away," "Nothing's
wrong, but don't tell anyone," or the unspoken message,
"Please emotionally deny what you physically see and how
you live."

Many of your mixed feelings and perceptions are based
on your observations that your alcoholic family was not
totally one way or the other. No dysfunctional family is
always negative or without some good times. On the
other hand, no healthy family is completely free of some
dysfunctional behavior or stressful times. Except, of
course, if you were raised by the Cleaver, Anderson,
Nelson or Brady family and visited your cousins, the
Waltons, on weekends. Perhaps you remember as a child
comparing your family to TV families and wishing your
family could be like that. Surprise, so did many children
who were raised in "normal" families.

We were and are a "looking-good" family and giving up that fantasy has probably been the most painful part of my recovery, but it's also where I've experienced the most growth and freedom.

Mary

In your alcoholic family you were probably exposed to both negative and positive behaviors from family members. Unfortunately in alcoholic families, as in other dysfunctional families, the negative experiences usually outweigh the positive ones. Thus your mixed feelings occur as you remember both. You might remember how your father was when he drank or how he could be verbally abusive. Yet, this was the same man who told you how beautiful you were and called you his special daughter. You may feel contempt for the alcoholism but love the person. You might have trouble admitting that your mom was alcoholic because, after all, this is *your* mother that you are talking about.

Although I know my mom had a drinking problem and it most likely played a large role in her death, I still cannot admit verbally that my mother was an alcoholic. I don't want and didn't want my mom to be an alcoholic. My mom was too special to be an alcoholic. I don't think I will ever be able to admit this fact.

Candice

Obviously what affects you negatively today about your childhood were the negative experiences you had. Regardless of the type of alcoholic family that you had, Ellen Morehouse tells us that most young children of alcoholics experience fears and concern over seven areas in their lives while they are growing up (Morehouse, 1982). These include . . .

1. Worrying about the health of the alcoholic parent.
2. Being upset and angry by the unpredictable and inconsistent behavior of the alcoholic parent and the lack of support from the non-alcoholic parent.

3. Worrying about the fights and arguments between their parents.
4. Being scared and upset by the violence or possibility of violence in their family.
5. Being upset by the parents' inappropriate behavior which can include criminal or sexual behavior.
6. Being disappointed by broken promises and feeling unloved.
7. Feeling responsible for their parents' drinking.

Margaret Cork reported in her research that children of alcoholics were most troubled by the arguing and fighting between their parents (Cork, 1969).

Not all alcoholic families are the same. As a matter of fact, not all members of any given alcoholic family will be affected the same. For example, if you have siblings, do they see your parents, the alcoholism, and their childhood experiences the same as you do? I find it amazing that I meet more adult daughters of alcoholics whose siblings will not admit to being adult children of an alcoholic. Although you may share much in common with other adult daughters, there are reasons why your childhood experiences in an alcoholic family may have affected you differently. These reasons may include (Ackerman, 1987) . . .

Your Age

Daughters who were born into an alcoholic family may have totally different perceptions and experiences than a daughter whose parent became alcoholic when she was 14. The younger you were when your parent became alcoholic, the longer you were exposed to practicing alcoholism and the higher the risk that you were negatively affected. (I wonder where they ever got the phrase "practicing alcoholism." Every alcoholic I ever met didn't need any more practice! So much for what I know.) Additionally, your developmental stage of childhood influenced how you perceived the alcoholism.

For example, a five-year-old sees only the behavioral effects of alcoholism, which she equates with drunken behavior. A 15-year-old can equate alcoholism with not only being drunk, but also with a variety of perceived motivations as to why the alcoholic drinks.

Children do not automatically recognize that the parent is alcoholic. As a matter of fact, many adult children will not accept it even now that one or both of their parents is or was alcoholic.

In childhood, recognizing that the parent has a drinking problem occurs in three stages. In the *first stage*, you began to realize that your house was different from that of your friends. However, just because our families differed this does not mean that something was wrong.

During the *second stage* you began to suspect that the differences between your home and other homes was something that you should cover up or deny because you did not want your friends to know.

In the *third stage*, you become aware of what the difference is, which is that your parent drinks too much.

According to the Adult Daughters of Alcoholics Study (ADOAS, 1988), on which this book is based, most daughters of alcoholics reached the third stage around age 13 (Ackerman, 1988). This does not mean that the daughter told anyone, but rather that she admitted to herself that she knew what the problem was in her house. After all, many adult daughters are admitting the alcoholism only now, long after their childhood experiences have ended.

However, other factors influenced when many adult daughters reached stage three. These were the gender of the alcoholic parent and whether they had two alcoholic parents.

For example, most daughters of alcoholic fathers reached stage three when they were 12 years old. Approximately 60% of the adult daughters had an alcoholic father only. Daughters of two alcoholic parents admitted the drinking problems when they were approximately 14 years old. This may be due to the fact that both parents did not become alcoholic at the same time, or if you had two alcoholic parents, you did not have a non-alcoholic role model to compare it to. Therefore, it may have taken longer to realize the inappropriate behaviors in your parents because they were both doing the same thing and it wasn't until you were exposed to other parental role models that you began to admit the differences. Only 20% of the adult daughters had two alcoholic parents.

Daughters of alcoholic mothers did not reach stage three until they were almost 19. This may be because women traditionally have developed alcohol problems at later ages than men, or that the daughter wanted to deny a drinking problem longer in her mother than in her father. Another reason would be that if you are an adult daughter of an alcoholic mother, you were much less likely to know someone else with an alcoholic mother since only 20% of adult daughters had an alcoholic mother as opposed to the 60% who had an alcoholic father.

Alcoholic Mothers, Alcoholic Fathers

Are daughters of alcoholic mothers affected differently than daughters of alcoholic fathers? You may have entirely different memories, perceptions and experiences of your childhood depending upon the gender of your alcoholic parent. Additionally if you had two alcoholic parents it is very possible that the effects of the alcoholism were not equally received. That is, you probably identified more with the alcoholism in one parent than with the other. This is not to say that one of the alcoholic parents did not affect you, but that you were more influenced by one or you derived more positive or negative feelings from one than the other. The impact and feelings of adult daughters of alcoholic mothers and fathers will be discussed more fully in later chapters. (No skipping pages. *Come back here!* Besides, you're likely to feel guilty if you don't read all of this.)

Contributing Others

While you were growing up was there someone special who you could share your feelings with about your family life? This could have been another relative, best friend, teacher, neighbor, or in some cases, your non-alcoholic parent. If you had someone who cared about you and your problems, she or he made a contribution to your life by helping you with your feelings. This special person allowed you to share the "family secret." You may not have solved anything together, but just being together with another person and believing that you were cared about and supported helped you.

Unfortunately only 13% of adult daughters indicated that they had someone to share their feelings with while they were growing up. Those who did have such a person in their lives were much less likely to seek treatment as adults than those who had no choice but to keep all of their emotions and feelings to themselves. If you had such a friend, the further you proceed in your recovery from your childhood the more you will realize how much she or he contributed to your life.

> I wish I could have had real parents. I've always wondered what it would have been like to have someone care about me and share my deepest hurts and secrets and successes.
>
> Nancy

Parenting Behaviors And Styles

Although one or both of your parents were alcoholic while you were growing up, what kind of parent were they? For example, how did the alcoholism affect the ability of the alcoholic to fulfill her or his role as a parent? On the other hand, how did the alcoholism in the family affect the ability of your non-alcoholic parent to fulfill the parent role? Was your father or mother totally incapacitated by the alcoholic drinking?

Many adult daughters expressed that their strongest feelings about their childhood were more associated with how the alcoholic behaved toward them than with the actual drinking. In other words, the parenting that you received or didn't receive can affect your memories about your childhood more significantly than those memories that are related to drinking only.

How the parent attempts to fulfill the role can affect the child. You may have had a parent who made an effort to be an effective parent, but was unable to break the addiction from alcohol.

> We felt that our father really did love us, he just wasn't very good at it. He messed up everything he tried, but he did try.
>
> Carol

Other daughters were convinced that the alcoholic or non-alcoholic parent would lie awake at night trying to think of what else they could do to oppress their daughter!

> And when our father used to get us up in the middle of the night and march around the house singing "Onward Christian Soldiers," it would be a school night and we would think that we should be able to sleep like normal kids. And, Mom please help us, come to our rescue, but she never did.
>
> Cathy

Not all parents, alcoholic or non-alcoholic, have the same behaviors or the same styles of parenting. If you had a parent who ignored you as opposed to one who attempted to overly control you, you were affected differently. Adult daughters indicated that the behavior they remembered most was that the alcoholic was verbally belligerent. This alcoholic parent was usually argumentative, verbally abusive and walked all over everyone's beliefs and self-esteem.

Other daughters stated that the alcoholic parent displayed behaviors that ranged from embarrassing them in front of friends to physically or sexually abusing them. It was found that 31% of adult daughters experienced physical child abuse, 19% were victimized by sexual abuse, and 38% witnessed spouse abuse in their families. These rates of abuse were three to four times higher than found to occur among women who were raised in non-alcoholic families. Clearly the daughter who experienced not only the alcoholic parent, but also abuse, was affected more and differently than the adult daughter of a non-abusive alcoholic.

> In my own recovery I found that I slowly experienced and found ways to express anger at Dad for his various abusive rampages while he was drunk. The surprise was that I had seen my mother as a victim all those years and never held her responsible for the hell my brothers and I went through.
>
> Valerie

Some adult daughters indicated that their alcoholic parent was passive and paid little attention to them or other members of the family. Others stated that the alcoholic pretended to be very carefree and that nothing was to be taken seriously. This might have been fine, according to the alcoholic's thinking, but it sure didn't work for too many adult daughters who adjusted to the alcoholism by taking everything in their lives very seriously.

As you might suspect verbal belligerence and offensive behaviors occurred more among alcoholic parents than did passive and carefree behaviors. Additionally those daughters who experienced the verbal and abusive attacks indicated that they were far more negatively affected by the parent than daughters of passive and carefree alcoholic parents.

Your Perceptions

Eighty percent of adult daughters perceived that having an alcoholic parent highly affected their lives. Twelve percent indicated that they were moderately affected and 8% believed that they were unaffected. What is the source of their perceptions? Are their perceptions the ones that they had as children or do they come from their experiences as adult daughters who see things differently now?

Your understanding of your childhood as a child may be totally different from how you see it now. Whatever most of us define as real, we usually react to as if it exists. Whether it is real or not, we respond to it based on our perceptions. All daughters of alcoholics do not share the same perceptions of their experiences. This section began by asking what was it like in your home as a child? However, what did you *think* about your family as a child? Did you perceive and believe that not only was something wrong in your family, but also that you were being affected? If you thought that something was wrong, did you know what it was or did you think it was you?

> When I was growing up, I just felt very lonely all of the time. I felt like I didn't have any friends, that life was passing me by and I was often depressed. I can't say that at the time I was experiencing it, I recognized it as being unnatural. You know I thought there was something wrong with *me*.
>
> Paula

It is very difficult to get an accurate and consistent perception of something when it is chaotic, constantly changing, contains mixed messages or when we are not able to understand what is happening. Many adult daughters admitted to being very confused as children, not only about the drinking, but also about how they should behave in their own families. Thus if you assumed that the parent did not have a drinking problem, then you would try to behave as if your mother was not alcoholic. However, this became confusing when you found yourself doing things to compensate or cover up for a condition that you wanted to perceive did not exist.

Our perceptions of having an alcoholic parent can depend upon several things. The first and foremost is denial. While growing up if you wanted to deny that your parent was alcoholic, you probably also denied that any problems from drinking existed. Or you denied the drinking by convincing yourself that any dysfunctional behaviors in your family had nothing to do with drinking.

Another way that our perceptions can be distorted is by minimizing. Such statements as, "It really wasn't that bad," "It didn't affect me," or "He isn't drunk, he just doesn't feel well," are all examples of attempting to minimize the impact of the alcoholism.

As a child how well did you understand what was going on in your family? In other words, did you know that it was alcohol problems or alcoholism that was causing the pain in your family? If you did not fully understand what was happening, you probably do not accurately perceive your situation. As a child, your uncertainty about the situation could explain differences in opinions about what occurred.

All of these reasons for different perceptions can explain why many adult daughters admitted that they recognized the alcoholism in a parent as a child or teenager, while other adult daughters indicated that they did not perceive the problem of alcoholism until they were adults.

> My mother was an alcoholic but I didn't know she was an alcoholic when I was a child. So for me, being a child of an alcoholic didn't start until I was about 15 years old. Before that, the experience was more of being a child in a family that was unloved and that I was a troublemaker and not wanted. Because of that I felt I was to blame when I did find out that my mother was an alcoholic.
>
> Renie

2

What Did You Learn
At Home Today?

What did you learn during your childhood? I am not talking about what you learned in school, but rather what you learned about yourself and especially what you learned from your family. Whether you were aware of it or not, the lessons that you learned from your family affected you, not only during your childhood, but remain with you today. In fact, according to the Keri Report on Confidence and the American Woman, approximately 40% of women stated that they got their self-confidence from their upbringing (1988). Your family-influenced childhood lessons have affected many of your values and opinions about relationships, intimacy, parenting skills, career choices and most importantly, your self-esteem.

As the daughter of an alcoholic, during your childhood you were learning three things simultaneously. One was how to grow as a child and a human being. Another was how to adjust to belonging to an alcoholic family. The third learning experience involved your development as a girl and a young woman.

Learning to become a child and a human being are referred to as normal developmental tasks. Many theorists, such as Erik Erikson, believe that humans progress through stages in their lives and at each stage the person is confronted with a particular task to work through (Erikson, 1963). Gail Sheehy in her book *Passages* writes that we all go through different periods or passages in our lives and each period has its unique emotions, characteristics and challenges (Sheehy, 1980).

Eight Stages Of Development

According to Erikson, the tasks involved in our lives occur in eight different stages. At every stage it is believed that we are faced with trying to resolve a particular conflict. If we are successful, we would achieve conflict resolution. As a child if you were not able to work adequately through a given stage or conflict, it is believed your task would remain unresolved.

Before we discuss each stage and its particular task a very important part of this theory should be kept in mind. It is believed that how well we do at one stage determines not only how well we have handled the task, but also that the new resolved skill will help us to complete successfully the next stage. Thus each stage becomes a prerequisite for the next.

Adult daughters often stated the sequence of the stages did not occur properly. Many adult daughters were forced to grow up too quickly or never experienced the emotions of childhood. Although this book is written to and about adult daughters, much of who you are, what you believe and how you feel was developed during your childhood stage. If the period of childhood did not influence us as adults, there would be no reason to have adult children's programs. Think of how nice it would have been as a child to tell your family, "I am a child and until all of my developmental and emotional needs are appropriately met, I will not be going on to adolescence!"

The eight stages of development can be divided into the periods of childhood, adolescence and adulthood. Remember that at each stage we are looking for a positive resolution to the normal conflict and if it does not occur, the opposite can happen.

Childhood Tasks

1. Trust Versus Mistrust

The development of trust in our lives is the first task and, according to Erikson, it is the most critical of all of the stages. It establishes the foundation upon which the successful resolution of all other tasks depend. As young children, if we were not able to develop a healthy sense of trust in ourselves and in others, Erikson believed that the opposite would develop and that we would become mistrusting. To develop trust in childhood young children of alcoholics, as well as all children, need to be exposed to trustworthy adults.

How much trust existed in your alcoholic family? Was the amount of trust related to the amount of drinking? The more drinking, the less anyone trusted anyone else. More importantly can you trust people today? It is often said that adult children are "either-or" in giving their trust. Either we refuse to trust anyone, or we give our trust too easily, which usually results in pain.

One of the most difficult forms of trust to learn as adult children is can we trust others with information about ourselves? This is a very scary form of trust. It involves risk because we are trusting that at a later time in our relationship the other person will not use what we have shared against us, to harm us. In most alcoholic families the silent rule about sharing information was — keep it to yourself.

> I didn't know what trust was. Every time I got involved in trusting at home, trusting that my mom wasn't going to

drink, or she was going to work her program, I was devastated when she didn't. So that just blew trust right out the window for me.

Veleta

2. Autonomy Versus Shame And Doubt

Children need to learn that they can do things for themselves and not be overly controlled. At the same time they need consistent guidance to be able to learn. If healthy balance between autonomy and belonging do not occur, a self-concept of inadequacy and shame develops.

Here comes that famous word known by every adult child, *control*. In most alcoholic families everyone is trying to maintain some control over an uncontrollable situation. For example, your father is trying to control his drinking, your mother is trying to control your father and (if you were a "good" child) you were trying to control both of them. Children in alcoholic families are overly controlled. Either others were attempting to control us too much or we were trying to control our families too much. It is doubtful that you were given the opportunity to develop a healthy sense of self-control. When this does not occur, shame develops and doubt about our abilities to exercise control over our lives begins to occur.

Control for me goes hand in hand with the fear of abandonment. When I was 16 years old, I had almost complete responsibility over my brothers and sisters and I didn't think anything of it. I thought it was perfectly normal to come home from school, go to the baby-sitters to pick up my siblings, feed them, clean house, put them to bed, wash their clothes and all that. It didn't seem to me to be abnormal, but I think my control issue started at 16 because everything was so bizarre. Everything was out of control. I would walk into the house and never know what to expect. Was it going to be war? Was it going to be a carnival? I never knew. So I ran off and got married. I found somebody who was very needy and married him. I was in control, 16 years old, and I had complete control.

Audrey

Do you ever feel like your life is out of control or that you are controlled by others against your will? Ironically, we often react to the lack of control by attempting to become controlling of others. Besides we believe one of the best ways to make sense out of chaos is to take charge. Who was in charge of your family while you were growing up? Was control equally or reasonably shared? More importantly, were you allowed your fair share of control in order to develop a healthy sense of autonomy?

3. Initiative Versus Guilt

Conflicts between your initiative and guilt feelings may have begun when your curiosity about the world was treated as inappropriate by adults. If your questions were ignored or hushed up and your normal childhood games were restricted, it is likely that you developed many guilty feelings without knowing the cause. In order for you to develop a healthy sense of initiative, your parents needed to maintain a balance between the rules and the amount of permission you were given for your behaviors. Parental consistency is the key to achieving this goal. Erikson believed that inconsistency did more harm than being too restrictive.

How did you handle the inconsistency in your house? Many adult daughters reacted by becoming overly conforming or people-pleasing. This often resulted in subjugating normal childhood activities. Another common pattern at this stage is when the child begins to imitate the behavior she observes in the adults around her. Needless to say, this lays the foundation for repeating inappropriate adult role models.

What makes you feel guilty today? If being yourself makes you feel guilty, you may have given up your normal childhood curiosity in exchange for inappropriate feelings about yourself. If you feel guilty unless you put everyone else first, you have sacrificed your normal interests and growth.

4. Industry Versus Inferiority

Always feeling inferior puts you at a disadvantage in every relationship you have.

Robyn

During this stage of our childhood it was necessary for us to develop a feeling of usefulness. Unfortunately in many alcoholic homes children begin to believe that they are useless or that their accomplishments are always second to the drinking problems. To accomplish this developmental task, it was important to have your parents express interest in your accomplishments. Merely doing most of the work in the house does not contribute to a personal sense of being useful for children. It contributes to a sense of being used, or of being valued only for what you do, not for who you are. When we are repeatedly rejected, we begin to feel that we are unlovable. Repeatedly being rejected equals lost self-esteem.

You know I had ways of getting attention, but it never seemed to be enough. I still had this sense of being alone. I remember a lot of times trying to get my dad's attention. I don't know if that was unnatural or what, but I remember thinking in grade school if I would just go to school and get hit by a car, someone would pay attention to me. You know, feeling like I should just die and then everybody would pay attention to me.

Ada

Adolescence Tasks

5. Identity Versus Diffusion

Remember your "reputation" in high school? Some would like to forget it. No one is more conscious of identity than a teenager. This is especially true because of trying to find a place to belong and wanting to fit in. The development of identity neither begins nor ends in adolescence, but rather begins to solidify.

It is difficult enough to grow through this process with all of the confusion of adolescence, let alone trying to accomplish it in the midst of mixed family messages and confusion. Developing a sense of personal identity becomes overshadowed by a negative family identity. When this stage of our lives has begun, carrying many unresolved issues from our childhood stages makes the task even more difficult.

> I was always ridiculed as a child and I always gave my power away to other people, to other kids. Whatever they said to me, I felt they were stronger, they were more important than I was. Whatever was said about me, I believed. I just isolated myself and just pretended like I was a tough little girl who didn't need anyone. And I'm still doing it.

> Barbara

6. Intimacy Versus Isolation

I consider developing the skills necessary to establish positive emotional intimacy as the most critical developmental task for children of alcoholics. Intimacy problems begin as people begin to push you away and reject you. The core of all intimacy problems is a fear of abandonment by others.

If you were successful at this stage, you emerged with a healthy sense of self-love and the abilities to like and genuinely love others. If this skill and emotional closeness was not developed, you probably became emotionally isolated from your own feelings and from people around you.

Another risk at this stage occurs when you confuse intimacy with something else. For example, constantly giving too much to others in hopes of getting something in return is not being intimate. This is especially true when you receive nothing in return, but keep trying because you feel that you are to blame for the lack of intimacy. This is not intimacy, this is being misused by others. Robin Norwood points this problem out repeatedly in her book *Women Who Love Too Much* (Norwood, 1986).

I never remember being hugged as a child. I never remember being told that they loved me or I was lovable. So I
never felt those things.

Sue

Adult Tasks

Although these are not childhood tasks, we will include
them since it is obvious that our childhood significantly
affected how well we can work through our adult tasks.

7. Generativity Versus Self-Absorption

Generativity is the ability to give beyond ourselves to
the next generation. It is the basis of our parenting skills.
To be effective parents it is assumed that all of the previous skills were learned correctly. However, we know
that one of the most frequently mentioned problems of
adult daughters is related to their concern about their
ability to be a healthy parent. A tremendous amount of
our attitudes and values as parents come from our childhoods, particularly from the role models we observed.

My biggest fear is that I will hurt my children . . . I will or
have been repeating the very same types of behavior, which
I felt hurt me, that my parents displayed.

Gayle

8. Integrity Versus Disgust

Integrity means we are accepting responsibility for our
own lives and that we do not blame others. It means that
we have learned to like who we are and what we believe.
It means that we have developed healthy self-concepts
about ourselves. I see integrity as synonymous with Abraham Maslow's concept of self-actualization, whereby we
truly become and live as we wish to be (Maslow, 1965).

Do you like yourself? Do you love yourself? Unfortunately, the most negative legacy of alcoholic families is
producing adults who do not like themselves. I would
argue that it is far more difficult to live with yourself if
you do not like who you are, than it was to live with an
alcoholic parent. We can and have tolerated harmful be-

haviors in others for a long time. However, when we do things that we do not like about ourselves, we can't stand it. This creates a great dilemma for most of us. We would like to have healthy relationships with others, but we don't like what we are offering them — ourselves.

The core of recovery is related to this last stage. Recovery is working through all of the previous stages and becoming the kind of person that we would like to be. It is recovering from alcoholism, from our developmental stages and from ourselves. It is the ability to look in the mirror and like what we see.

As you read through these developmental stages did anything become obvious to you about yourself or about adult children? It did to me. Look at the characteristics that supposedly would result from unresolved tasks. Lack of trust, shame and doubt, guilt, feeling inferior, identity confusion, isolation, lack of parenting skills and not becoming the kind of person you would like to be are all a result of unsuccessful conflict resolution.

Where have you heard these characteristics before? Aren't these characteristics some of the same ones so often mentioned by adult children? Could it be that not having a healthy childhood contributed to these problems for adult children? Well, the answer is obvious, isn't it? Yet too often we look only at the alcohol or the drinking to explain problems for adult children, not at the childhood experiences themselves and how they have contributed positively and negatively to your growth.

After awhile you learn the subtle difference
Between holding a hand and chaining a soul.

And you learn that love doesn't mean leaning
And company doesn't mean security.

And you begin to learn that kisses aren't contracts
And presents aren't promises.

And you begin to accept your defeats
With your head up and your eyes ahead
With the grace of a woman or man
Not with the grief of a child.

And you learn to build your roads on today
Because tomorrow's ground is too uncertain for plans
And futures have a way of falling down in mid-flight.

And after awhile you learn
That even sunshine burns if you ask too much.

So you plant your own garden and decorate your own
    soul
Instead of waiting for someone to bring you flowers.

And you learn
That you really can endure
That you really are strong
And you really do have worth.

And you learn . . .
And you learn . . .
With every failure
You learn.

                                        Kara Di Giovanna

3

These Are The Things
I Learned

She was never there for me because she was either drunk
or drugged. I saw things as a little girl I should never have
seen or done because of my mother and what I was forced
to do.

Pat

The developmental problems discussed in the previous
chapter are not the result of only one explanation, such as
the failure to work through developmental tasks. They
are a combination of many things.

As an adult daughter, the most significant impact on
your normal development was living with the crisis of
having an alcoholic parent. In other words, did living in
the crisis of an alcoholic family affect your ability to
establish your normal developmental growth? What happened to you as a result of growing up while living in a
crisis situation?

In Chapter One, I identified age as one of the factors that explains why adult daughters are not all the same. It is interesting to speculate whether or not a particular problem for an adult daughter is related to not only her age when the alcoholism developed, but also the developmental task she was trying to work through when the alcoholism began.

For example, are adult daughters who have problems trusting others more likely to have been born into an alcoholic family or to have had the alcoholism develop when they were very young and trying to establish trust which was the first developmental task of their lives? Or are adult daughters who have intimacy problems more likely to have had a practicing alcoholic parent when she was a teenager and struggling to establish intimacy skills?

Adjusting To Your Family

Lee Ann Hoff in her book *People in Crisis* believes that one of three things can happen to a person as a result of living through a crisis (Hoff, 1984). The first implies that the person in crisis attempts to reduce the anxiety and tension by developing patterns of negative behaviors. Many adult daughters have indicated that they adjusted to the situation by engaging in behaviors, such as becoming isolated, withdrawn, overly controlling, or people-pleasing, as a response to the alcoholism. At the same time, they were aware that their behaviors were not only ineffective in stopping the alcoholism, but also that they were sacrificing their own health and emotional needs.

The second response to a crisis assumes that the person in a crisis can return to a pre-crisis state. If this occurs the individual would remain the same as she was before the crisis developed. Additionally, it means that the crisis would have no lasting effects. Unfortunately, very few adult daughters indicaced they were able to return to a pre-alcoholic condition. If it were possible, one condition that would need to happen would be that the alcoholic would become sober. Unfortunately most studies reveal that only about 10% of alcoholics get sober. Therefore, this pre-crisis state is not likely to occur and it is very doubtful that your exposure to alcoholism would have no effects on you. Remember, only 8% of adult daughters indicated that they were unaffected by the alcoholism.

The third outcome of a crisis occurs when the person not only survives the crisis, but emerges with behaviors and strengths that she would not have developed if she had not lived through the crisis. Obviously, all three of the outcomes could occur for adult daughters.

I believe that a combination of the first and the third response is what occurs for the majority of adult daughters. This occurs when both positive and negative behaviors and emotions develop as a result of the exposure to the alcoholic parent. Most of the time, however, the negative effects begin to dominate or you are so conditioned to focus on your negative behaviors, you seldom consider your assets. Obviously, any assets learned from an alcoholic family were painfully learned.

A crisis equals danger, but it also equals opportunity. With intervention and recovery, the painful lessons of childhood can become the foundation of your growth and strengths as an adult.

For example, if you had no choice as a young girl but to take care of yourself because others couldn't, you now know that you *can* take care of yourself. As stated in the Preface, I see adult daughters, as well as all children of alcoholics, as survivors. In order to survive you *have* developed strengths. You may or may not be aware of them, or you may not have considered that many of your behaviors do have potential benefits. It is ironic that sometimes we do things before we have "discovered" what we have done.

Being an adult daughter is a very conflicting place to be especially if you become aware of this later in life. On the one hand you feel you finally found out why you've been different all your life. You're also angry that so much has passed, but you're also happy, you've survived, made something of yourself and finally achieved "peace."

Toni

Gender Identity

While you were handling the above tasks in your life, you were also developing your gender identity as a girl and young woman. Although we are advocating role changes for both females and males in our culture, we are not attempting to abandon our concepts of femininity and masculinity. I believe that rather than moving towards gender role changes, we are probably attempting role convergence. This would occur when either gender can fulfill a role with an equal amount of competency and respect and still maintain gender identity.

Another point about gender socialization involves what happened to you as a child and what you expect from yourself today. For example, your childhood may have occurred during a period in our society when gender patterns were very distinct and you emerged with an unconscious set of female expectations. However, as an adult woman these patterns may no longer be applicable. If the patterns of your childhood and your adulthood are different, this creates a dilemma between how you were raised and how you would like to be as a woman today. This same type of problem exists when you consider how you adjusted as a child to an alcoholic family and how you would like to be today as an adult. Your childhood behaviors may have carried over into your adulthood and kept you from growing. Unconsciously, you may still be reacting to others as if you were still living at home. Both of these situations, your gender socialization and adjusted childhood behaviors, can create many mixed messages that keep pulling you back unconsciously. These messages started in childhood, but what were they?

What happens to the gender development of young females in the alcoholic family? In our society we have experienced "expressive" role socialization for women.

Historically, this pattern has resulted in women developing emotionally expressive, nurturing, other-directed, and supportive roles (Zelditch, 1956; Sanford, 1985). Does exposure to an alcoholic parent alter this pattern?

Claudia Bepko in her book *The Responsibility Trap* believes that gender development in the alcoholic family is intensified. For example, rather than changing typical gender patterns for girls in the alcoholic family, the daughter is often expected to become even more understanding, more nurturing and more oriented to meeting others' needs than are daughters raised in non-alcoholic families. She states that "females learn that they must be nurturers who never ask for nurturing" and "women are socialized to be emotionally over-responsible . . . messages about appropriate adult dependency needs are contradicting and paradoxical — women are to be both dependent and primary emotional caretakers, but are never to express their own emotional needs" (Bepko, 1985). Certainly clinical observations and the many stories shared by adult daughters support this theory. Many adult daughters have stated that they became the expressive center of their family and that they felt that it was their responsibility to ensure that all family matters were under control and emotionally satisfied.

> I constantly told everyone that everything was okay. It was not my father's fault, just give it to me and I'll take care of it.
>
> Ruth

A common pattern seems to emerge for many adult daughters. This pattern involves the intensifying of her gender role identity to the point that it becomes dysfunctional for meeting her own needs. She is at risk in the alcoholic family of becoming a person who is out of balance because she is disproportionately expected to meet the needs of others. This causes problems for working through her own developmental goals. Many of the very characteristics that she values as a female, such as her ability to identify emotionally with issues and people effectively, can place her at risk of being used by others due to their inability to handle their own problems. Many daughters have consistently expressed their pain over being placed in a position of surrogate parent or spouse when all they wanted to do was to have a "normal" childhood.

Perhaps you can identify with some of these positions in your own life. If you felt that you were responsible or you were to blame for most of the activities in your family then you overly identified with your perception of your responsibilities. Lynn Sanford, co-author of *Women and Self-Esteem*, believes that women, more than men, are more likely to hold themselves personally responsible when something goes wrong (Sanford, 1988). For example, she believes that if something goes wrong for a male, he is more likely to look outside of himself first for the reason why. He will look for *external* reasons for these problems. However, she believes that women are more likely to look *internally* or blame themselves first when things go wrong before they will blame others. Unfortunately, alcoholic families are professional breeding grounds for these types of patterns for daughters.

Childhood Lessons

Looking back on your life, how well have you handled your learning tasks of human development, adjusting to an alcoholic family and becoming a woman? Are you aware of how each area influenced the other? Are you aware of positive and negative lessons that were learned in childhood?

We may not always be aware of the things that we have learned. While lessons are being taught, we usually learn two things at the same time. We learn the intended lessons, which is what was supposed to happen, and we learn the unintended lessons which are unanticipated consequences of the learning process.

For example, as a child you learned to read. Someone spent time with you for the express purpose of teaching you to read. The fact that you have progressed this far in this book means that you succeeded in learning how to read. However, what did you learn about reading itself? Did you learn that you like to read or did you learn that reading is something that you *must* do. Not only did you learn reading, but you learned opinions about reading.

Therefore, during your childhood you learned many intended and unintended lessons from your alcoholic family. Normal human development should include the intended lessons of your life. Many unintended lessons are learned from living in an alcoholic family. These lessons can be very painful and last a lifetime unless they can be unlearned or changed from liabilities in childhood to assets in adulthood.

Did you unintentionally learn any of the following lessons as a daughter in an alcoholic family?

- If I can control everything, I can keep my family from becoming upset.
- If I please everyone, everyone will be happy.
- It is my fault and I am to blame when trouble occurs.
- Those who love you the most are those who cause you the most pain.
- If I don't get too close emotionally, you cannot hurt me.
- It is my responsibility to ensure that everyone in the family gets along with each other.
- Take care of others first.
- Nothing is wrong, but I don't feel right.
- Expressing anger is not appropriate.
- Something is missing in my life.
- I'm unique and my family is different from all other families.
- I can deny anything.
- I am not a good person.
- I am responsible for the success of a relationship.
- For something to be acceptable, it must be perfect.

All of the messages above have one thing in common which is that they have negative consequences for your own growth and recovery as an adult daughter. These childhood lessons become imprints or beliefs that you have about yourself and they begin to dictate your expectations of yourself and your behaviors. If you examine these lessons closely, you will see that living by these "rules" will lead to a life out of balance.

However, you have survived and somehow you have maintained some balance in your life. Therefore, there must be other lessons you have learned that have served you well or have allowed you to survive. Again, you may not be fully aware of these other lessons. As a matter of fact, for many adult daughters not only are these lessons unintended, but also in many cases, they are undiscovered. These lessons are called the painfully positive lessons of your childhood. In other words, they can have positive results for you, but they have been learned as the result of experiencing pain.

Why are these painfully positive lessons undiscovered? Usually it is because when we are in the middle of a crisis, we do not have the time or the awareness to look for benefits. We are too busy surviving. An unspoken motto for many children of alcoholics might be, "Survive now and heal later."

While living in an alcoholic family, how many of us thought that anything positive was happening or that anything positive could possibly come from our experiences? Don't get me wrong. I am not saying that being raised in an alcoholic family is a positive experience. I do, however, support Lee Ann Hoff's idea that some people come through a crisis and learn behaviors and strengths that they would not have developed otherwise. If we do develop any benefits from a crisis experience, it is much more likely that we become aware of them after the crisis is over. Therefore, as an adult daughter you are now in a position to determine whether or not you have learned anything from your negative childhood experiences that you could use to your benefit as an adult.

For example, I believe that many adult daughters learned the following lessons and they are in the process of not only discovering that the lessons occurred, but also they are discovering the best parts of themselves. **Can you identify with any of these undiscovered qualities?**

- I am a survivor. I can survive.
- I have developed competencies in many areas of my life.
- I can handle crises.
- I have a good sense of empathy.
- I can take care of myself.
- I am not easily discouraged.
- I can find alternatives to problems.
- I am not afraid to rely on my abilities.
- I can be healthy when others are not.
- I do have choices.
- I can be depended upon.
- I appreciate my inner strength.
- I know what I want.
- I am a good person.
- I may not be perfect, but parts of me are great.

I have learned to be grateful for the experiences of my childhood. I know that I am a survivor and that I have incredible strengths that served me well . . . I love me. I am excited about the future, and I am excited about TODAY.

Karen

To Be Or Not To Be A Good CoA

Another challenge in your childhood years you could have experienced involved the dilemma of having a choice between two options. These were, you could either adapt to the alcoholism and try to become a "good" child of an alcoholic or you could try to have a normal childhood and have your developmental needs met. Unfortunately, it was difficult to do both.

If you were a good child of an alcoholic (CoA), then you would have engaged in many of the behaviors that led to the development of the negative lessons learned above. To be a good CoA, you were called upon to deny the alcoholism and other family problems, subjugate your developmental needs, hide your emotions, please others, pretend you were happy and be a "perfect daughter." These are not the behaviors that produce happy childhoods, let alone healthy adults.

On the other hand, if you tried to have a "normal" childhood, this was not likely to occur either. To accomplish a healthy childhood you needed others around you to be able to successfully fill their supportive roles. Most members of an alcoholic family are so emotionally drained, they are unable to meet a child's needs on a consistent basis.

Therefore if you tried to become the perfect daughter, you were denied your own needs. If you tried to develop and have the same experiences as children from non-alcoholic families, you quickly discovered that you were severely limited in your attempts to be normal. Either way, the outcomes were painful. However, if you were like most adult daughters, you probably tried to do both. Obviously, some adult daughters were able to do some of each more successfully than others. Regardless of how successfully you played both roles, we know that it caused pain, emotions to be denied and feelings that your life was out of control. These two lessons of childhood, like all of your other lessons, are somewhere inside of you today.

Your Childhood Spirit

Erikson tells us that the greatest crime of all is breaking the spirit of a child (Erikson, 1963). Inside of all of us is a childhood spirit. For some adult daughters this spirit has been neglected, abused and bruised, but it has managed to endure. Other adult daughters are very much aware that the spirit is emerging from the clouds of childhood, dusting itself off, and stating to the world — I am alive. This spirit of childhood is that part of all of us that wants to experience and enjoy life to the greatest of our potential. It is that part of us that constantly reminds us to take the risks, feel the emotions, reach out for warmth and communicate with the inner parts of ourselves that have been silenced too long. It is your childhood spirit that tells you that you will not have this day again, use it for all that it is worth. It is your childhood spirit that tells you that your life is not a rehearsal.

If you are not in touch with your childhood spirit as an adult, this does not mean that you do not have one. It means that your spirit has been neglected or denied and more importantly that it is currently not available for your recovery. What could cause your spirit to be absent? Typically, we look for the cause by asking, "What happened to you as a child?" We are looking for the ways in which you were victimized. Certainly, adult children were the victims of many things as a child. However, the greatest pain for many adult children may not be due to what happened to them as children, especially if they were not aware of the many forms of victimization that occurred. I believe that the greatest pain for adult children occurs not when you realize that you have been victimized, but rather when you become aware of what you have missed.

What did you miss as a child?

For example, if your parents were very withdrawn, you missed being nurtured. If your family was violent, you missed living without fear. If your father ridiculed you, you missed acceptance. If all of the energy in your family centered on the alcoholic, you missed feeling loved.

Many adult daughters have admitted that something is missing in their lives. Why is something missing? Because something is missing! Maybe their childhood spirit is missing. Discovering what it is and how to get it is part of recovery. Learning to discover what you missed in childhood is also a lesson from childhood. However, it's easier to see what you missed as a child now that you are an adult.

If you can learn from all of the lessons we discussed in this chapter, you can learn and discover that your childhood spirit is alive and well. It is hiding in your adult body. Yes, the period of childhood is over, but the spirit of childhood is available today. You have learned many lessons, survived much pain, and developed many skills. The true lessons of our past lie not only in what we have learned, but also what we have remembered that can help us grow today.

"Most of what I really need to know about how to live and what to do and how to be, I learned in kindergarten. Wisdom was not at the top of the graduate school mountain, but there in the sandbox at nursery school.

"These are the things I learned: Share everything. Play fair. Don't hit people. Put things back where you found them. Clean up your own mess. Don't take things that aren't yours. Say you're sorry when you hurt somebody . . . Learn some and think some and draw and paint and sing and dance and play and work every day some.

". . . When you go out into the world, watch for traffic, hold hands and stick together. Be aware of wonder . . .

"Think of what a better world it would be if we all—the whole world—had cookies and milk about 3 o'clock every afternoon and then lay down with our blankets for a nap. Or if we had a basic policy in our nation and other nations to always put things back where we found them and cleaned up our own messes. And it is still true, no matter how old you are, when you go out into the world, it is best to hold hands and stick together."

                                                Robert Fulghum

4

Alcoholic Mothers, Pains Of Endearment

As a child it seemed like my mother was almost always angry or extremely loving. I never knew when I came home which it would be. Either she might be warm and loving or she might be cold and hostile. It was scary to live in a house like that. You were out of control. You never knew what to expect. I got to the point where I would isolate myself and try to make myself invisible if I knew I wasn't doing something that would be approved of, or something that I would be accepted for . . . She didn't really spend a lot of time with me or share a lot of her life with me. I never really knew why. I thought it was me.

Meriam

Adult daughters of alcoholic mothers indicated that having an alcoholic mother taught them a variety of often

---

All of the quotes in this chapter are from adult daughters of alcoholic mothers.

confusing and painful lessons. The majority described their experiences as filled with anger, disgust, disappointment and devoid of bonding and nurturing as they were growing up. It was much more apparent that adult daughters of alcoholic mothers were more "attacking" in their comments, than were daughters of alcoholic fathers.

On the other hand, there were a few adult daughters of alcoholic mothers who wanted to deny even more emphatically that their mother was an alcoholic and wanted to protect her. These adult daughters did not want to accept that their mother could be an alcoholic and tried to remain close to them despite the drinking.

> Just because my mom was an alcoholic she was not a "bad" person. She was always there for me and did everything and more that a mother is supposed to do.
>
> Janine

Adult daughters of alcoholic mothers, therefore, shared a variety of childhood lessons that they learned, based on whether or not the daughter was angry with her mother or tried to protect her.

The following lessons were shared by adult daughters of alcoholic mothers . . .

- I am angry with my mother.
- I wanted to love my mother but she and her behavior kept pushing me away.
- I learned to be disappointed and disgusted with my mother and I have difficulty respecting her.
- I learned how to be responsible for my mother's duties and I resented always being in charge.
- I was denied information about my own sexual identity, how to be a woman and how to prepare for my future roles.
- I was taught unhealthy ways to relate to other people.
- I experienced poor parenting skills and I am unsure of my own parenting skills.
- I find it difficult to trust other women.
- I felt abandoned and let down.

• I am not sure of how to give and receive nurturing because I was not nurtured.

If you had an alcoholic mother, chances are you felt even more isolated than did adult daughters of alcoholic fathers. If your mother was an alcoholic, it is very likely that you have different issues than do daughters of alcoholic fathers.

Did you ever feel that at least daughters with alcoholic fathers can find other daughters to talk to about their problems? Statistically, we know that only one out of five adult daughters had an alcoholic mother. We are not sure of how many women alcoholics there are in the United States, but we do know that there are many double standard reasons for greater denial of alcoholism in women than in men. If you are an adult daughter of an alcoholic mother, you have probably found it very difficult to even read information about yourself since most studies on adult children seldom compare the differences between sons and daughters of alcoholics, let alone daughters of alcoholic mothers as opposed to alcoholic fathers.

If we want to understand the impact of gender differences on adult children of alcoholics, we need to consider not only the gender of the child but also the gender of the alcoholic. In the study of adult daughters on which this book is based, I did not find significant differences between daughters of alcoholic mothers and alcoholic fathers, regarding the degree to which either group identified with characteristics of adult children. (Characteristics of adult children will be discussed in a later chapter. I'm not going to tell you which one because you will be skipping around again. Oh, all right, they're in Chapter Six. I felt guilty for not telling you. How's that for codependency?) The overall scores between daughters with alcoholic fathers and mothers were about the same, but when you examine which characteristics and behaviors each group identified with, you will find differences. In other words, the groups differed on what bothered them more, based on which of their parents was alcoholic.

Statistics, therefore, did not tell the whole story, but listening to adult daughters' perceptions of the differences filled in many gaps.

Through interviews and clinical observations, there appears to be strong differences between daughters of alcoholic mothers and alcoholic fathers on such things as their levels of emotions, what problems they identified for themselves, their attitudes about the alcoholic parent and their recovery issues.

Adult daughters of alcoholic mothers shared that they were affected very strongly in seven areas of their lives because of their mothers' drinking. Some of these areas related directly to their relationships with their mothers while some areas related more to their own self-esteem or their abilities to relate to other people. As you read these concerns of adult daughters, you will be inclined to think many of the problems are common in a lot of mother-daughter relationships. This is true, but it is the degree to which they exist and how they have developed due to alcoholism that makes them unique and more difficult for adult daughters. This is another example of how normal interaction patterns are altered by alcoholism.

The seven most commonly mentioned issues for daughters of alcoholic mothers were role models, relationships, parenting, identity, trust, trying to please and shame. We will discuss each of these in the order of which they were mentioned the most by adult daughters of alcoholic mothers.

Role Models

It was not surprising that adult daughters of alcoholic mothers most commonly mentioned role-model problems. Our gender identifications traditionally come from identifying with people of the same gender. Daughters of alcoholic mothers consistently stated that they were angry, disappointed and confused by the role performance of their mothers. Some of this anger may have been directed inward and created additional problems for the adult daughter.

For example, one of the behaviors that was modeled by their mothers was how to drink. It was no surprise that we found the highest rate of concern was over their own alcohol and drug usage.

The inability of their mothers to fulfill responsibly their roles as a parent bothered many adult daughters. This was evident when the adult daughters stated they did not feel they had received proper nurturing or maternal support. In fact, many felt that the roles between them and their mothers were reversed. They felt they did not receive anything from their mothers, but were constantly asked to take care of them.

> I wanted comfort and love from her, but she was either angry, resentful, irritable or drunk and needing to be taken care of, put to bed, etc. I had and have lots of feelings of disgust for my mother as an alcoholic.
>
> Mickey

The inability of their mothers to fulfill their responsibilities led many daughters to share their resentment at having so much responsibility of their own at such an early age. They often stated they were forced into taking over the female role in the house. "I had to become the mother" was often repeated. Unfortunately, this put many of the adult daughters at high risk for incest, too.

> I had to take over the female roles in the family—caring for younger siblings, cleaning, cooking and sometimes being Daddy's sexual partner.
>
> Beverly

Many adult daughters of alcoholic mothers silently were asking, "What do you do without having been taught and emotionally supported?" These adult daughters answered hopefully, "The best you can."

Relationships

Not having a healthy relationship with their mothers was the most common relationship problem mentioned by adult daughters of alcoholic mothers. These daughters shared their concerns about not knowing how to relate to their mothers, no longer wanting to relate to them or feeling totally dominated by their mothers.

Mom was a closet drinker. I always knew something was wrong, yet couldn't place my finger on it. I was always attempting to reconcile with her but could never quite make it. How could I use her as a role model when I knew she had a problem? When is what she says valid and when is it not?

Jane

Other daughters stated that they now found it very difficult to interact with and trust other women as a result of their interactions with their mothers.

I have difficulty being friends with other women because I do not trust or believe that a woman values you as a friend. I always feel that women are the "enemy." I idolize the female, but I never find anyone "perfect."

Joyce

A common theme among some adult daughters of alcoholic mothers was anger with their mothers for indirectly teaching them to tolerate abusive male relationships. This may be due to the fact that almost half of all alcoholic women who enter treatment have been the victims of abuse in their relationships. If you witnessed your mother in an abusive relationship, did you unknowingly develop any attitudes that put you at a high risk for tolerating abusive males? Some adult daughters thought so and they were angry with their mothers for teaching them to be tolerant of such abuse.

I want to forgive my mom for teaching me to accept emotionally and verbally abusive men into my life. Mom accepted inappropriate behavior from my dad and I learned to do the same.

Cher

Parenting Skills

Did you learn any parenting skills from your mother? Adult daughters of alcoholic mothers stated that either they did not learn any skills or that the ones that they learned were negative.

> I was 36 years old and my mother had been dead for three years before I could convince myself I might possibly be a good mother . . . . My mother used to tell me she hoped I never had kids because they were such horrible ingrates. . . . I feel as if she cursed me. She used to tell my brother and me if we ever did anything she didn't like, she would have us put in reform school or a mental hospital. . . . My mother has been dead four years, but I still have a hangover.
>
> Claudia

Responses from adult daughters of alcoholic mothers about parenting range from not wanting children at all to wanting to be the perfect parent. Many adult daughters stated that they wanted to be there for their children because their mothers were not there for them. However, such statements as, "I don't want any children," "I don't know how to parent," "How can I nurture my children when I have not been nurtured?" "I do the same things my mother did and I hate it," "How do I relate to my own daughter?" indicate the difficulties shared by adult daughters of alcoholic mothers about their own parenting skills. Their messages carry a painful question: How do you do it, when you haven't seen it?

Identity

Having an alcoholic mother raised many identity issues for adult daughters. "How do you develop your sexual and feminine identity?" was the most frequently asked question. Most adult daughters expressed that they did not receive positive gender modeling from their mothers. They did not feel they were exposed to conditions to develop an appreciation for their own femininity. This often resulted not only in poor self-concept, but also about being a female. Intimate discussions and questions about sexuality never occurred for many adult daughters.

> I have become aware that in rejecting my mother's alcoholism, I rejected her and did not embrace all that it means to be a woman and feminine as well . . . . I felt emotionally abandoned. We never had any mother-daughter talks.
>
> Kathleen

Trust

As stated earlier many adult daughters admitted to having problems trusting other women. This appears to be related to not being able to trust their mothers and equating their mothers as indicative of all women. Other daughters felt that their trust problems were more related to themselves. They did not feel comfortable trusting their own feelings and believing that they perceived things accurately. It is as if others held the conditions that established or destroyed trust in their lives. It became a no-win situation for adult daughters of alcoholic mothers who learned that they did not trust themselves and they could not trust their mothers either.

> I would go to bed and trust that everything would be okay in the morning. In the morning I would wake up and hold my breath until I heard my mother's words. If they came out pleasant, I took a deep breath, deep sigh of relief, and then I could get on with my day.
>
> Lynda

Trying To Please

Did you ever feel inadequate because you tried so hard to please someone and they were never satisfied? If so, you can identify with the adult daughters of alcoholic mothers who shared this concern. Not only did many adult daughters find themselves forced into taking over many of the duties of their mothers, but also they were chastised for not doing it right. Adult daughters shared that they often felt emotionally trapped because they admitted they tried to please someone who caused them anger.

It is like being on a merry-go-round of whoever gives away the most is the best, except that you keep going in circles. We know that one of the most mentioned concerns for adult daughters is riding the "I have to please everyone" ride. It is one thing to try to please others and be appreciated, but it is extremely painful to try and please someone who not only denies your support but also tells you that you are not good enough. No matter what I do, *it* is not good enough, soon becomes *I* am not good enough.

Shame And Fear

Adult daughters often expressed that they felt more shame having an alcoholic mother than an alcoholic father. This may be just another example of the double standards in our society, but it still does not reduce the painful feelings for the adult daughter.

Adult daughters indicated that they went to great lengths to cover up their mothers' drinking. This is validated by the finding that adult daughters did not want to admit having an alcoholic mother until they were almost 19.

What was the greatest fear of adult daughters of alcoholic mothers? You guessed it. It was growing up and becoming just like their mothers. Becoming an alcoholic, repeating parenting patterns and developing poor relationships were the greatest fears for adult daughters. Many of the adult daughters expressed that they had become aware of their mothers' unhealthy behaviors only when the adult daughters started to do them themselves.

> When the heat is really on, my mother switches into "fuzzy" as I call it — gives erroneous responses to direct questions, seems confused and intellectualizes at a preschool level. Horror of horrors, I do the same thing and I hate it.
>
> Lisa

It is obvious that if you had an alcoholic mother, you experienced much pain and received little support. Besides the issues mentioned above, one very noticeable fact stood out. Few adult daughters of alcoholic mothers mentioned their fathers. None of the daughters indicated that they could count on their fathers to help or offset the impact of their mothers' alcoholism. We know that only 10% of men will stay with an alcoholic spouse. However, of those who stay, they do not appear to be able to help their daughters with the pain of having an alcoholic mother.

If you had an alcoholic mother, your feelings of extreme isolation, issues of sexuality, doubts as a parent and self-doubt are justified. Unlike daughters of alcoholic fathers, you are more likely to be confronted with your own gender issues in your recovery and you are more likely to be angry with your alcoholic parent.

Your greatest challenge in recovery will be to become your own healthy role model. However, you do not have to do this alone anymore. Look for healthy women to be around. Let their health surround you and support you. Allow their role-modeling to show you that there are healthy ways to relate to yourself and others. There are ways in which you can value your identity and more importantly yourself. As you begin to grow healthier, your anger towards your mother will grow weaker. Yes, your mother was an extremely influential and important woman in your life and she dominated your childhood. Childhood is over, but is her dominance and example over? Who is the most important woman in your life now? *You are!*

> I overflow with hope to know that beyond the angry feminist, beyond the silent housewife, beyond the temple prostitute, beyond the fearful little girl, there is a woman emerging. She is vulnerable and strong, vocal and receptive, active and inner, a mother, a wife, a person. She knows how to cry, to love, to dance and to forgive.
>
> Cindy

5

Alcoholic Fathers, Daughter Dearest

Dad was a happy person when he drank. He would play with me and I could have anything I wanted. I learned early how to "wrap him around my finger" because I was "Daddy's girl." Today he is sober, but I still have a hard time dealing with him as he does not want to talk about what it was like when I was growing up. It's like he has resolved things, but I'm not given the same opportunity.

Debbie

When I do workshops around the country on adult children, I always address gender issues. If possible, I divide the audience into groups. Each group focuses on specific gender combinations such as alcoholic mother-adult daughter, alcoholic father-adult daughter, alcoholic

All of the quotes in this chapter are from adult daughters of alcoholic fathers.

mother-adult son, etc. The largest group is always the alcoholic father-adult daughter. Most of the time this group is so large that it is divided into smaller groups. After watching this disproportionate interest among adult daughters of alcoholic fathers, I was beginning to wonder if alcoholic families specialized in having daughters.

But as we discovered women are more willing to support the growth of the children of alcoholics' movement and appear to be more willing than adult sons to support their own growth. On the other hand, we know that we have more alcoholic fathers than alcoholic mothers in this country. Additionally, we know that 90% of non-alcoholic spouses will remain with an alcoholic male, usually due to a lack of viable support alternatives. Therefore, the strong interest of adult daughters of alcoholic fathers is not surprising.

I don't know if adult daughters of alcoholic fathers are more aware of their concerns than adult daughters of alcoholic mothers, but they were much more willing to talk about them and to share their feelings more openly. This may be due to finding it easier to talk about your father than your mother, not feeling as isolated as adult daughters of alcoholic mothers or that having an alcoholic father is a more common experience.

If you are an adult daughter, chances are your father was the alcoholic. Did having an alcoholic father in your childhood leave you with specific feelings, issues and lessons? According to the many adult daughters of alcoholic fathers that I interviewed, it did.

Can you identify with any of these lessons that were shared by other adult daughters with alcoholic fathers?

- I still want to understand my father. I still want his acceptance and approval.
- I want to love him, but I hate what he does.   ·
- I have a low opinion of marriage and relationships. I fear I cannot find a successful relationship.
- I am aware that I have issues with my non-alcoholic mother.

- I have difficulty relating to males positively.
- I learned to tolerate too much inappropriate behavior from males.
- Am I good enough to be loved?
- She who gives away the most is the best.
- I find "healthy" males boring, and the "wrong" ones available.
- I never got enough attention.
- I missed not having a "father-daughter" relationship.
- I have difficulty expressing anger to my father.

Besides the above lessons, I observed some other differences about adult daughters of alcoholic fathers. It is important to remember that although many of these issues might be found in many types of father-daughter relationships, it is again the degree to which they occur and how they are dominated by alcoholism that makes them unique for adult daughters of alcoholic fathers.

For example, I noticed the way that adult daughters talk about their alcoholic fathers was much different from how adult daughters talk about their alcoholic mothers. I am not referring to the fact that both groups identified different issues, but rather *how* they talk about them. As you recall, adult daughters of alcoholic mothers expressed much anger, resentment and appeared more "attacking" when talking about their mothers. Adult daughters of alcoholic fathers, however, appeared to be more "defensive" when talking about their fathers and expressed a need to understand his behavior.

Although many of their fathers engaged in highly dysfunctional behaviors and caused much pain for them, I still found a desire to establish a relationship with him in most cases. With some adult daughters this was not the case. They were extremely angry with their fathers and wanted to separate from them as much as possible. However, when an appropriate father-daughter relationship did not occur, as was usually the case, I found that many of the adult daughters held themselves partially responsible for the lack of a positive relationship. In essence, alcoholic fathers were not held totally responsible for their behaviors by their daughters, but alcoholic mothers were held accountable or attacked for everything. Reasons for treating an alcoholic mother differently may be due to our unfair practice of blaming-the-mother syndrome, it is another example of our punitive double standards. We feel more comfortable accusing our own gender than the opposite one, or there is a greater tolerance among adult daughters for their fathers' behavior.

Daughters' Need For Fathers' Approval

I wonder, however, if another reason might be because many adult daughters expressed a need for their fathers' acceptance and approval. Therefore, we are less likely to focus negatively or consistently attack those whose approval we want. After all, this could become a reflection on you.

For example, you are not likely to go around publicly condemning someone and then express your need for their approval. This would raise the question of what kind of person are you. Therefore, if you want their approval and you want to feel comfortable about it, you must minimize their negative behaviors. This is kind of an emotional trap, isn't it? Sounds to me like mixed messages. This could become overwhelming if you think about it. (Scarlett O'Hara had to be a CoA. How else could she have invented, "I'll think about it tomorrow.")

For example, as a young girl your alcoholic father provided you with many mixed messages, such as "I love you, go away and leave me alone" or "You are expected to love me and I am expected to do what I want." Now that you are an adult your relationship with him can still be dominated by mixed messages.

> My dad to me was mixed messages: "I love you, provide for you, call you Dolly and yet I cannot talk with you or have an exchange of conversation. I cannot accept anger or conflict, yet I come across as angry and in conflict with each person in the family, including you."
>
> Renee

As an adult you can now carry these mixed messages inside of you. You might be feeling that you want to acknowledge the pain of his alcoholism on your life, but if you do, you no longer believe him to be a person worthy of approving you. However, his "approval trap" was very strong and silently controlled you. You no longer want to be emotionally controlled by him, but he only related to you in a controlling manner. Thus whatever relationship you may have, means if you want to stay close — stay quiet.

Why would you want approval from someone who harmed you? Because you were being controlled. Most alcoholic fathers were found to be very controlling, either emotionally and/or physically. Wanting the approval of someone who negatively affects you is the epitome of being in a controlling relationship. Again, you were probably caught in a mixed message or a no-win relationship. How do you get close to him and not be controlled, especially if the only behaviors that he approved of were pleasing him? As I'm sure you are aware, it is very difficult to separate emotionally from a powerful and controlling father.

However, his control may not be the only form of control that you are feeling. You may be silently controlling yourself because you are holding yourself partly responsible for the quality of your relationships with your father. Therefore, if your relationship is poor and you believe that you are responsible, whether true or not, you are suffering from "justifiable emotional homicide." Thus you are being controlled externally by him and internally by your self. When this happens, the mixed messages of childhood become internalized. They become part of us. It is no wonder that as adult children we have difficulty overcoming these messages. These erroneous messages are given to us. We internalize them, then give them to ourselves. Wouldn't it be nice if we could give them back, or tell the sender to keep them to himself as we are too healthy to listen!

Another difference I found among adult daughters of alcoholic fathers that I did not observe among adult daughters of alcoholic mothers, was that alcoholic fathers usually created "longing" in their daughters. Longing is a plea to be accepted and loved. Longing is a hunger. It is an emotional need that is not met. Above all, it is not love. Many adult daughters expressed a longing for a positive father-daughter relationship and were very aware when this need was not met. Longing may explain why many daughters defended their fathers' behaviors. Emotional hunger can distort your perceptions. Therefore, many daughters did not want to see their fathers as they were, but rather how they should be. This idealized version of fathers remained strong with many adult daughters.

> In my case I wanted him to be my "knight in shining armor." He did not live up to this and up until now, no man has ever been able to live up to my ideal.
>
> Jennifer

Relationship With Non-alcoholic Mother

While growing up with an alcoholic father, what did you think about your mother? Discussing their relationship with the opposite parent was another major difference between adult daughters of alcoholic mothers and fathers. Daughters of alcoholic mothers seldom mentioned their fathers. However, many adult daughters of alcoholic fathers openly discussed their relationships with their mothers and many of the problems in that relationship.

Relationships with their mothers ranged from an appreciation for how much their mothers helped offset the problems of an alcoholic father, to holding their mothers accountable for the family problems. It was frequently stated that many of the behaviors of their mothers established negative role models for them. Adult daughters were very aware of how their mothers' reactions to an alcoholic spouse negatively influenced their opinions not only about their mothers, but also about spouse relationships, expectations in marriage and their attitudes about how to relate to males. This was especially true if their mothers were highly co-dependent and engaged in many dysfunctional behaviors. In fact, research indicates that when a non-alcoholic parent is highly co-dependent the effects on the children are the same as if the children had two alcoholic parents (Obuchowska, 1974).

> Many of my resentments and worst memories are with my non-alcoholic mother who was sicker than my dad. I have no real relationship with my dad and that makes me sad. I believe this has caused problems in my relationships with men.
>
> Susan

Although the above are behaviors I observed myself about adult daughters of alcoholic fathers, the following issues were also mentioned. These issues focused on relationships, role confusion, intimacy, a sense of self, sexual abuse and perfectionism.

We will discuss each, beginning with the one most frequently mentioned.

Relationships

Does the relationship that you had as a child with your father affect your relationship with males today? According to the adult daughters represented in this book, it does.

Relationship issues for adult daughters of alcoholic fathers were divided into two categories. One is the relationship that you had with your father and the other is about your adult male relationships now. For many adult daughters these are not two separate issues, but rather one which affects the other.

> My father rejected me. I was 48 years old before he ever gave me a birthday gift or card and then I wondered why he was doing it now. In my marriage to an alcoholic, I have found the same rage for my husband that I have for my father.
>
> Mary Lou

What is or was your relationship with your father? Do you feel as if you had two relationships? One was the actual relationship with your father and the other was your idea of how your relationship ought to be? If so, you are like most adult daughters.

One of the major problems of alcoholic fathers, according to their daughters, was that they never talked. They communicated very little and developed a feeling in their daughters that their fathers never really "knew" the daughter. He often lacked parental compassion and was emotionally unavailable.

For example, can you count on one hand the number of meaningful father-daughter conversations that you had? You may have wanted these to occur as often as possible, but he was not emotionally prepared or available.

This non-communicating man managed to exercise a great amount of influence on his daughter. Actions are stronger than words is an understatement when describing many alcoholic father-adult daughter relationships. If you are like most adult daughters, however, you have probably hung in there with him and you are hoping that you will someday be able to have a more positive relationship.

What kept you hoping? You eventually began to expect very little from him and thus any attention took on significant meaning. Many adult daughters stated that they eventually believed that they "understood" their fathers better than anyone else. This often included defending his behaviors to others.

Understanding him might have resulted from your abilities to read correctly and anticipate his moods and behaviors. This skill is developed in many children of alcoholics at an early age because your physical or emotional survival each day is dependent upon your intuitions of how you should react. Unfortunately, these are the same behaviors for the development of co-dependency.

Fathers often supported this understanding behavior in their daughters. Usually he was not aware of her motivation, which was that he was not being an effective parent. Therefore, she would do what she could to establish some kind of a relationship. If you did this, you probably engaged in a lot of pleasing him behavior. If you could please him by your actions or words, he at least communicated something to you. He would interpret your behaviors as not pleasing him, but understanding him. Usually he used this in arguments with your mother by stating that, "At least *my* daughter understands me."

His motives for accepting your behavior were usually selfish and to maintain his denial of alcoholism. Your motives were probably to get closer to him and this was one of the few ways. If your father deprived you of attention and approval, you might have searched for ways to get it. Some daughters eventually gave up and others are still trying.

The legacy of an alcoholic father for most adult daughters can be found in their opinions about males or in their male relationships. In fact, when it came to discussing relationships with adult daughters, relationship problems with other men were expressed more than those with their fathers.

> It's so strange, almost indescribable. My father is an alcoholic. My husband is not, but I still frequently find myself waiting for my husband (almost expecting him) to begin to display some of the behaviors my father did. Sometimes it seems like I'm pushing him to be like my father whose behavior I hated.
>
> Kelly

As you might suspect, most adult daughters expressed concern about how to relate to males due to the influence of their fathers.

What are your opinions about male relationships? What are your opinions about males? Are you attracted to healthy males or do you find them boring? Are you attracted to unavailable males? Are husbands something that you think you should have, but you're not sure what for? Your answers to these questions may be based on how your father directly or indirectly fostered your ideas about men.

The greatest fear expressed by adult daughters was that they would wind up in a relationship with a male who was similar to their parents. This was not surprising given that only 11% of adult daughters rated their parents' relationship as above average. Adult daughters, therefore, shared their concerns about males on such subjects as . . .

- How to relate to controlling men
- Understanding healthy relationships
- Distrust of males
- Looking for Father in their relationships
- How to have a male friend
- No male is good enough
- Seeking unavailable men
- Addicted to relationships.

Role Confusion

Adult daughters of alcoholic mothers mentioned their exasperation over the poor role-modeling they observed in their mothers. Adult daughters of alcoholic fathers, however, shared that their fathers were often poor role models, but talked about their own role confusion more. In other words, they stated that they were very unsure of their roles in the family. This was largely due to the vagueness of emotional and physical boundaries of interaction in the family between their fathers, their mothers and themselves. Did you ever feel caught in the middle in your parents' relationship?

Many adult daughters expressed role confusion because with an alcoholic father, they often felt that they were taking the place of their mother.

For example, some adult daughters stated that their mothers were emotionally absent and full of resentment towards their fathers. This situation caused the fathers to expect that their daughters understand them and support them. In many ways the fathers responded to their daughters in what I call "emotional incest."

Emotional incest occurs when a parent shares information with her or his child that should be shared with the spouse. Thus many adult daughters talked about becoming their fathers' emotional confidant. This type of interaction produced confusion for many daughters about where her role as daughter stopped and her role as adult emotional supporter started. This was not an appropriate role for a child or a young woman.

> Mom rejected Dad sexually in their mid 40s, so Dad and I became emotionally incestous. I need to learn to set emotional and sexual boundaries with men. I need to be assertive with my needs towards men and not fear losing them.
>
> Tamara

Intimacy

"I have a lack of self-esteem with men. I fear failure in my relationships. I am looking for a man to love me. I lack closeness with men and I sacrifice myself to keep a relationship." Do any of these sound familiar to you? These statements reflected many of the concerns of adult daughters about their ability to achieve intimacy in their relationships. There was no doubt that many of the adult daughters held their relationship with their fathers accountable for these problems.

> My search for intimacy? I spent a lot of years of my life, especially adolescent years, looking for a boy to love me, but not sexually. My father never talked with me. He never really talked to me at all, but he loved me. I know that he did . . . I had to reach out to external sources for acceptance, guidance and strength.
>
> Colleen

Did you feel that your father really did love you, but was not good at expressing it? If so, what did you learn about intimacy? Did you learn that it was difficult to express? Did you learn that you could express it, but that it was okay if he didn't? Did you learn that your intimacy needs were not as important as his? It seems that intimacy under these conditions is like living on a one-way street. You can leave your house and get somewhere, but you can't get back. Your father may have loved you, but you may not have developed the most important ingredient required for intimacy, which is the ability to receive it.

> I am furious because my father made me his emotional spouse. I could never be me, never be sad or angry or have any negative feelings because he was so selfish and needy.
>
> Marla

Are you afraid of intimacy? Fear of intimacy was another problem shared by adult daughters. They stated that they had developed very low opinions or expectations about intimacy. Others indicated that they equated being intimate with not being in control and being too vulnerable. Fear was also based on not being accepted by their fathers or having their attempts at intimacy rejected.

> What I realized was that I had developed a fear of intimacy, and that subconsciously I was keeping my husband at a distance. I was afraid of becoming too close and giving myself to him completely because in the back of my mind I knew that I would be rejected. So if I didn't give myself completely, then I couldn't be completely hurt.
>
> Marian

Sense Of Self

> I think you have to accept yourself as a woman, and probably more importantly, a person. You have to realize that you are important as yourself and not an extension of another person.
>
> Sherri

It was not uncommon for adult daughters to question their feelings about themselves. Alcoholic fathers often instilled in their daughters problems of self-concept and' self-esteem. Adult daughters of alcoholic fathers shared that they secretly found it difficult to value themselves, to feel good about themselves. This may explain the strong need for approval and acceptance from their fathers. When approval or acceptance is withheld, we are left to our own interpretations about ourselves. If we do not have an adequate internal sense of self-worth, we are not sure about our own performances. When this occurs, we look outside of ourselves for our identity and worth. Constantly wanting your father's approval in order to feel good about yourself keeps you externally focused.

> My father was a silent, shy, passive alcoholic so I never knew how I stood with him. I usually thought his thoughts about me were negative. I was surprised when he told my husband I am his favorite child. I am the oldest of four.
>
> Michelle

How do you feel about meeting your own needs? Are you comfortable meeting your needs or do you feel more comfortable meeting the needs of others? Do you feel guilty if you think about yourself first? Having an overly developed sense of guilt was found among many adult daughters of alcoholic fathers. These guilty feelings were related to feeling guilty about who you are, your self-worth and even your sexuality. We develop a strong sense of self when all of our emotional parts are well integrated. For example, when you feel good about your ability to believe in yourself, your abilities to contribute to others, your abilities to take care of yourself and who you are as a person, you have developed a well-balanced sense of self. Many adult daughters stated that their interactions with their fathers kept them off balance.

> My father destroyed my healthy sexual image of myself. When I was a teenager, 12 or 13, and started to like boys, he said they were like dogs sniffing around if they showed any interest. I became ashamed of my sexual feelings and later felt pretty worthless. I got into a sexual affair with a boy at college because I didn't have any regard for myself. I did a lot of things in college I am ashamed of and realize now that it was because of total lack of self-esteem. I still haven't completely forgiven myself.
>
> Dawn

Sexual Abuse

Unfortunately, almost 20% of adult daughters indicated that sexual abuse occurred in the families while they were growing up. These adult daughters were raised in double jeopardy and experienced twice the amount of victimization. All of the fear, rage, anger and emotional impact of being sexually abused dominated their childhoods. Although all adult children feel that their childhoods were taken from them, sexually abused adult daughters shared that as well as a lost childhood. Identity, personal boundaries, emotional support and personal security were also stolen.

If you were sexually abused as a child, your recovery takes on so many other dimensions besides having an alcoholic parent. Sexually abused adult daughters felt totally betrayed by their fathers and emotionally abandoned. Research findings indicate that the closer the sexual abuse victim is emotionally to the perpetrator, the greater the emotional damage. Most sexually abused adult daughters indicated that they didn't know where to turn for help while growing up. Additionally, due to all of the dysfunctional behaviors in their alcoholic families they felt their isolation even more.

> The sexual abuse started when I was age 12. It lasted for approximately one year. I thought I was doing something to cause what was happening. My father told me if I did not keep quiet, he would leave my mother. The confusing part was my father was really a nice man when he wasn't drinking. I would not sleep at night until I knew he was home and passed out. I was afraid to tell anyone. At age 13, I planned to kill my father. I thought about how I was going to do it when he was on top of me. He came home drunk one night and came into my room. He would always call me in a mean voice "Laurie." I pulled the gun from under the covers and shot him. I hit him in the shoulder. I'm 44 years old now. My father died three years ago just before Christmas. He always claimed that he shot himself. He never came into my room again. No matter how I rationalize or understand, I have to

live with the fact I shot my father. I was the oldest and the
only girl.

Laurie

Perfectionism

Are you a perfectionist? Absolutely not, I just do things
better than anyone else. Sound familiar? Always wanting
to please makes you do the best that you can. However, it
also means that you are never satisfied unless it is the best.

If you wanted your father's approval, how did you get
it? By being the best? Or if you didn't get his approval,
was it because what you did was not good enough?

> I followed my father's career. I was a high achiever, went
> on to law school, worked in the office trying to do everything
> perfectly . . . It was probably the best way for me to get his
> attention and his approval. That's why I adopted everything
> he thought and believed because then I knew I was safe. If I
> agreed with him, then he was happy.

Marcy

Perfectionism develops from a desire to want to be
perfect. Perfect in whose eyes, yours or someone else's?
Usually we mean someone else's. Have you ever done
something and someone points out how wonderful or
perfect it is? What do you do? Agree or show them the
flaws that you know exist? If you do this you want to be
perfect for someone else. For adult daughters of alcoholics
this person was often your father. You may have tried to
live up to his ideal of the perfect daughter.

Overcoming perfectionism is not easy, especially if you
want to do it perfectly (just kidding!). Why does perfectionism have such a hold on so many adult children? It
may be because we have not learned enough ways to be
valued or to feel good about ourselves. Therefore, if we
are perfect in the eyes of someone else, we are at least
acceptable to ourselves. Does this make sense to you?
Perfect sense, thank you.

I always did the best I could do but it was never good enough. If I got a "B," I should have got an "A". If I cleaned the house real good, my dad would move the furniture and say I didn't clean behind the furniture so it wasn't good enough. So in my own life everything is in place because then that means that I've got it all together and things are good. If things are out of place, something is wrong.

Althea

In spite of the many issues, in spite of the pain, in spite of his behavior, in spite of how he treats your mother, do you still want a father-daughter relationship? Would you still like to have his acceptance and approval? Would you like to know that he loves you for who you are and respects you? If your answers are yes, you are like the majority of adult daughters of alcoholic fathers.

Perhaps, however, the most important question is . . . if you cannot or will not be able to establish this relationship, will you go on and become as healthy as you can? It will not be easy. Even when we change, we want others' approval. Herein lies your hope. Although your father's approval was and still is important to you, if it is not available or it is an unhealthy form of approval, there are many other sources and many other people who can provide you with a healthy sense of approval. This does not diminish your desire for a relationship with your father nor make you a less than perfect daughter. Rather, it makes you a more healthy human being to know that you have alternatives, that you have the potential for growth that cannot be limited by someone else's inability to offer their approval. Of all the people in your life today, who is it that is most likely to give you the healthiest and the most honest approval about yourself and your behaviors in order for you to grow? *You are!*

I am the most important one whose love and approval I need. Let go of looking for love and approval outside yourself and give it to yourself . . . Through this I have found a deep underlying strength. I have an ability to take care of myself on an emotional level. The ways in which I have done this may not have been the most growth-promoting, but if I've learned those behaviors, I can learn others . . . I have found a lot of positives waiting under the surface and if going through this is how I came to these realizations, that's fine. As long as I know more of my own worth now.

Elizabeth

6

Two Alcoholic Parents: Don't Add, Multiply

I'm an adult daughter of two alcoholics who attempts to take care of the world. I know that I must let go if I'm to live. I take life too seriously. I'm afraid of having my own kids. I don't know how to be a parent. My spouse drinks heavily. I find myself in a vicious circle. I'm continuing the patterns and I'm tired. Yet I don't know if I have the courage to change. I know the steps. Like a good ACoA, I've read all the books but this time I don't know if I can fix it.

Winifred

Almost everything that was said in the last two chapters about having an alcoholic mother or an alcoholic father applies to adult daughters with two alcoholic parents.

All of the quotes in this chapter are from adult daughters of two alcoholic parents.

However, one thing which can be said about adult daughters of two alcoholic parents is that their experiences were much more intense. According to adult daughters with two alcoholic parents, they consistently reported that their problems were much more critical, they had greater feelings of despair and felt even more unsure of how to recover than did adult daughters of one alcoholic parent.

If you are an adult daughter of two alcoholic parents, I am sure that you will identify with many of the problems of all adult daughters. However, just as adult daughters of alcoholic fathers or mothers have their own unique problems and concerns, so do daughters of two alcoholic parents.

For example, as a daughter of two alcoholics you represent only one out of every five adult daughters. Therefore, you are likely to experience even stronger feelings of isolation and uniqueness. Daughters with only one alcoholic parent may have had a non-alcoholic parent who was able to help them. It is unlikely that you received such help and therefore you had to rely on yourself even more. Did this make you feel even more isolated?

> How do you teach yourself self-esteem? How do I encourage myself? Will I ever believe I'm okay? Thank God for the ACoA meetings and the literature on the market.
>
> Vickie

According to Carol Williams and her work with alcoholic families, in your family there was a much higher risk of physical child abuse. Thus, you may have been victimized physically as well as emotionally. Additionally, she found that the quality of child care was lower in families with two alcoholic parents (Williams, 1983).

I found that adult daughters of two alcoholic parents did not identify with the problems of both parents equally. It was more common for adult daughters to identify more strongly with the issues of the opposite gender parent. This does not mean that you do not have concerns or that you were not affected by your alcoholic mother, but that adult daughters of two alcoholic parents focused more on the problems associated with their father's drinking. Some adult daughters, however, stated that they found it very difficult to separate their problems between their mother's and their father's.

My mother is now deceased which gives me a different perspective on my problems. Strangely enough, my problems stem more from my relationship with my father. I'm an only child of older parents. Did he expect me to make it all better for him, too? He's a daily drinker. During later years we did talk about mother's problem when she wasn't eating properly. I think I'm still trying to have a relationship with him — such a waste!

Florence

Rather than discuss the same issues which were found in adult daughters of one alcoholic parent, in this chapter we will focus on those issues for adult daughters of two alcoholic parents who were more intense and obviously more painful.

For example, I found that adult daughters of two alcoholic parents identified more strongly with the following six problems than did adult daughters of one alcoholic parent.

Concerned About My Relationships

Having two alcoholic parents produced lower levels of emotional satisfaction for adult daughters in their lives, than did having one alcoholic parent. If you had two alcoholic parents, how well have you handled your relationships? An indicator of relationship problems was that adult daughters with two alcoholic parents were less likely to get married, but much more likely to get divorced. Many adult daughters stated that they were afraid of relationships because they never witnessed any parts of a healthy one.

As I answered these questions from an adult daughter

perspective, I realized how difficult it was to separate the problems that resulted from the fact that my parents would have been dysfunctional even without the alcohol. They came to each other with their marriage already damaged and were unable to help each other grow. The alcohol added another dimension.

Myrtle

Concerned About My Children

Fear of parenting for adult daughters of two alcoholic parents was very high. Many of these daughters expressed their fear of not only not having children at all, but also of how to raise healthy children with limited parenting skills. Wanting to be a "perfect" parent was also a major concern.

This adult daughter was so tired of parenting my parents that I vowed not to have children and did not.

Patricia

Other concerns of adult daughters about their parenting involved being too controlling, not knowing how to parent, lack of consistency and not being able to nurture their children. Although these concerns were shared by almost all adult daughters, they were especially evident for adult daughters of two alcoholic parents.

My biggest fear is that I will hurt my children and that I will or have been repeating the very same behaviors, which I felt hurt me, that my parents displayed. I am overly aware of my emotions and feelings and I try hard to help my children express theirs.

Eileen

Concerned About My Relationship With My Parents

How well do you get along with your parents? How well do your parents get along with each other? Both of these questions were important concerns to daughters of two alcoholic parents. On the one hand, adult daughters were saying that in spite of all of the problems, they would still like to have a relationship if possible. Adult daughters of two alcoholic parents were much more sensitive to the absence of a good relationship with their parents. Good times between you and your parents or even one of your parents were too few, if at all.

Absence of criticism was the closest thing to praise I ever received.

Chooch

Do you still find yourself hoping or doing things that you think will help your parents to get along with each other better? Marital problems in alcoholic families are a norm, but in cases where both spouses are alcoholic, it is an understatement. Daughters with two alcoholic parents experienced even more marital tension and problems. Many of the daughters believed if they could just get their parents to get along better, it would help tremendously. Does this sound familiar to you? It is the same pattern that many young children of alcoholics follow. While you were young, did you do things hoping that you could help improve the relationship between your parents? For many adult daughters of two alcoholic parents, they are still trying and still hoping.

Concerned About My Own Alcohol Or Drug Use

Higher rates of alcohol and drug problems were found among adult daughters of two alcoholic parents. Daughters with alcoholic mothers were also at a greater risk for alcoholism than were daughters of alcoholic fathers (Niven, 1984). However, having an alcoholic mother not only placed the adult daughter at a higher genetic risk, but also having an alcoholic father combined to place her at a greater role model risk. Additionally, Sharon Wilsnack found that women's drinking patterns are strongly influenced by the drinking patterns of their husbands, siblings and friends (Wilsnack, 1982). Again, this places adult daughters of two alcoholic parents at higher risk due to the fact that so many of the adult daughters wound up in a marriage with an alcoholic spouse.

> I am a recovering alcoholic of two years. I have been in individual therapy for three years and I have just started a women's ACoA therapy group. Through my AA recovery, therapy and my last relationship, I am finally becoming aware of my patterns in relationships and that I need to focus on me now. It is very frightening to be alone, but I have hope. I have run in every way possible from myself and now I am beginning to stop.
>
> Lee

Concerned About My Spouse's Use Of Alcohol Or Drugs

It is commonly believed that adult daughters disproportionately marry alcoholics. This statement is partially true, but is also biased. Although it is true that many adult daughters find themselves in an alcoholic marriage, they did not find themselves an alcoholic to marry! Very few women ever marry an active alcoholic. Adult daughters disproportionately marry males who *become* alcoholic. Unknowingly, adult daughters may marry males who are at a very high risk for alcoholism. This appears to be especially true for adult daughters of two alcoholic parents. Given these high risks, it is no wonder that you may be in a relationship with someone who is addicted or someone who is very controlling. Perhaps you are in a relationship with a high risk male, such as a son of an alcoholic. Regardless of the situation, we know that adult daughters of two alcoholic parents are highly concerned about the alcohol and drug use of their spouses.

> It has been like wearing blinders. I put them on in order to survive, but they prevented me from seeing alcoholism developing in my husband or being able to talk with my daughters about it.
>
> Mimi

Concerned About How To Get
My Parents Sober

As is the case with all adult daughters, wanting to get their parents sober is a strong concern. For adult daughters of two alcoholic parents this was even stronger. As I have traveled and shared with many adult children I have heard over and over the desire to get the parent sober. However, adult children cannot get sober for their parents. This does not mean that they sure don't try. However, if you could get sober for your parent, I am sure that you would have done it years ago. I do not doubt your sincerity, but I accept the reality that you cannot get sober for them. Do you accept this, or are you still taking on the responsibility for getting them sober?

Besides the above areas of concern, remember that adult daughters of two alcoholic parents also share the problems of intimacy, role confusion, sexuality, perfectionism, identity, trust and trying to please others that were found among adult daughters of alcoholic fathers or mothers only. If you are an adult daughter of two alcoholic parents, your road has been far more difficult, your issues more intense and you are more likely to be emotionally exhausted from the experience.

As an adult daughter of weekend alcoholic parents, I feel very emotionally burned out. I have a hard time dealing with personal problems in my life. I feel very physically and emotionally tired, which is not usual for someone who was always very active and ready to attack problems head on. I feel cheated in that my childhood was stolen from me and I had to take on adult responsibilities at such an early age.

Diane

Adult daughters of two alcoholic parents have shared that their recovery has depended upon their abilities to rely on their own inner strength. At the same time they have stated that they are very aware of the need to be around healthy people to help draw them out and to provide healthy role models.

Be patient and compassionate and respect your own growth process. Make conscious decisions to be 100% responsible for your own life and focus on being in mutual relationships which nurture and support. Allow yourself to feel your feelings, especially anger, and create a nurturing supportive network of people for yourself. Look for information, but trust your inner voice for your life's direction and purpose.

Toby

PART TWO

Co-dependently Yours

7

Me, Myself And I: How Well Do You Know These People?

Are you *really* different from other women? If so, what is different about you? Is it your personality, behaviors, characteristics or do you just "feel" different from other women without knowing why? On the other hand, if you do not believe that you are different from other women, and you are an adult daughter, how have you overcome many of the feelings and characteristics commonly associated with adult children?

Both of the above questions have one thing in common. They both ask, "How well do you know yourself?" Are you aware of how your childhood experiences have influenced your behaviors and personality characteristics? Do you like what you know about yourself or have you become the person you never thought you would be?

In this chapter we will discuss and discover your personality characteristics and the extent to which they are similar or different from women from non-alcoholic families and from other adult daughters. Why bother to know your characteristics or behaviors? If you would like to change or recover from your childhood, it would help to know how and where you have been affected. It is easier to change yourself when you know what you are working with.

> After recently reading a book about adult children, I identified so unbelievably and completely with characteristics of adult children of alcoholics. . . . I realized for the first time and understood where, and how it had affected me. Oh, I cried, but to see how it had affected me and where my characteristics fit in, was overwhelming. I think the tears that I felt were partly of relief. . . . I had some reason for feeling lonely.
>
> Madeline

Adult Children Characteristics, Do They Describe You?

Since the early 1980s clinicians have observed certain personality characteristics that they attribute to adult children of alcoholics (Perrin, Woititz, 1983; Ackerman, 1985). The number of these characteristics typically has been around 20. As I began to examine these characteristics, I found myself wondering whether or not they are found in other adults.

For example, supposedly taking yourself very seriously is an adult child characteristic. Aren't there other adults who take themselves seriously? Isn't a certain amount of seriousness part of being an adult?

If adult children really are different from other adults, I do not believe it is possessing particular characteristics that makes them different, but rather the *degree* to which they are found in adult children. Therefore, it is more correct to say that these personality characteristics can be found in all adults, but are overly developed in adult children. And overdevelopment of some of these particular characteristics can place you at risk for developing certain problems in your life.

To what extent do you identify with any adult children characteristics? Let's look at the 20 most commonly described characteristics about adult children and apply them to you. In my work with adult daughters I was able to measure the extent to which they exist or don't exist for women from non-alcoholic families and for adult daughters. Additionally, I was able to identify seven different "feelings" that the 20 characteristics measured. In other words, if you possess certain characteristics, how does that make you feel?

Additionally, many of the characteristics are related to each other. For example, the characteristics of taking yourself very seriously and difficulty having fun are associated with each other. Therefore, if you identify very strongly with certain characteristics, you probably have very strong feelings about your needs as an adult child.

How obvious to you are your characteristics and how strongly are you aware of the feelings that accompany them? Ask yourself the following questions in each section using this scale, 5 = always, 4 = often, 3 = sometimes, 2 = seldom, 1 = never.

Feeling Isolated

_____ I guess at what is normal.
_____ I feel different from other people.
_____ I have difficulty with intimate relationships.

Two of the most common feelings expressed by adult daughters were that they felt unique and at the same time emotionally isolated from others. These two feelings support each other. The more unique and different from other people you feel, the more isolated you become. Without adequate role models, you were on your own to judge how "normal" people behaved in their relationships, friendships, parenting and intimate exchanges.

I didn't ever see myself as a game player. I tried to watch what other people did in order to maintain relationships. My role models were a mother, who was wrapped up in her drinking, and a father, who was too wrapped up in my mother. I didn't really know what a normal relationship was. I would watch other people and mimic them. Literally, I would see what worked for the people on TV or in a movie or my healthy friends and I would actually mimic them. And I could never figure out why it didn't work for me.

Teresa

Inconsistency

_____ I have difficulty following projects through to the end.

_____ I look for immediate as opposed to deferred gratification.

_____ I manage my time poorly and do not set my priorities in a way that works well for me.

Do you sometimes feel as disorganized as your childhood? How can we be so controlling and yet feel inconsistent? If you spent a lot of your time meeting other people's needs, there was not much time for you. Finishing up your own projects and working on your own priorities were either done last or in a hurry when you had a "spare" moment. Rarely were they done in a logical or comfortable atmosphere.

Another reason for your inconsistency may be related to the usual amount of chaos that accompanies life in an alcoholic family. Judy Sexias refers to the alcoholic family as the "disorderly-orderly family" (Sexias, 1986). Everyone is trying to put consistency into an inconsistent environment. In most alcoholic families this was not possible. Besides I have never experienced an orderly and consistent crisis, have you?

Self-Condemnation

_____ I judge myself without mercy.
_____ I have difficulty having fun.
_____ I take myself very seriously.

Are you tougher on yourself than other people are? Do you have two sets of standards? One set is accepting and kind. This set is applied to other people. The other set is excessively demanding and unforgiving. This set is applied to you.

If you are very self-critical and take yourself too seriously, you are at risk for self-condemnation. This occurs when we are so overly judgmental about our own behaviors that we can never please ourselves. Even when we do well, we don't believe it if we view ourselves negatively. The core of self-condemnation is having a low self-esteem. Self-condemnation results from never feeling that you are good enough and that it is your fault. Therefore since it is your fault, you condemn yourself. This was found to be even more apparent among adult daughters of alcoholic fathers than mothers (Berkowitz, 1988).

Take it easy. Who made you the judge and jury about all of your behaviors? I know, you did. However, you don't have to have an "emotional" trial on everything you do which results in the same verdict — guilty. Guilty of what? Trying your best? No, if you are guilty of anything, it is not taking enough time for yourself and not appreciating yourself enough. Remember, G. K. Chesterton tells us the reason that angels can fly is because they take themselves lightly.

I'm just now learning to have fun. That has meant taking some risks too. It's difficult to sit down and write a list of even 10 things that I would do that I consider fun things. A lot of things that I tend to see as fun things, I would do alone.

Marge

Control Needs

_____ I over-react to changes over which I have no control.
_____ I am either super-responsible or irresponsible.

Do you have a strong need to be in control at all times? Have you ever thought of what it is that you want to control? The desire for control among adult daughters was obvious to most adult daughters. However, what they wanted to control was not so obvious. That is, you have this feeling of needing to be in control at all times, but you are not sure of what it is you are trying to control.

Control issues for adult daughters were most likely to surface in one of three areas. One, many adult daughters wanted to control situations and their surroundings. This form of control is very closely related to your childhood, especially if you were the type of daughter who was trying to reduce the chaos in your family by taking charge of everything. Thus if you were in charge, you were in control. If you were in control, you could make order out of chaos. Do you still feel a need to be in control of situations?

The second form of control occurs when you want to control relationships. You either do this by your willingness to do more than your share in a relationship or by wanting guarantees from people that they will "never leave you." For example, if you do 75% of everything that needs to be done to maintain a relationship, you may believe that you are in control. However, when this occurs, aren't you the one who is being controlled? It is unfortunate, but many times we believe that we as adult children are very controlling when in fact control is an illusion. If we were in control why would so many of these dysfunctional things be happening in our lives?

> I would try to control the outcomes and in turn I became very much co-dependent because I tried to control the other person — not only the outcome of the situation, but also the person. It was very draining, but I didn't have to look at myself.
>
> Hannah

The third type of control occurs when you want to maintain total control over your emotions. This may have worked as a child in the alcoholic family for a while, but it sure doesn't help your adult well-being. What do you do with your emotions? If you totally control them, does that mean that you do not express them? Probably so. Therefore, do you control your emotions or in reality do they control you?

Wanting to control your emotions can be based on the fear that if you allow yourself to express them, too much may come forth and you will be out of control. Besides you may have heard all of your life "don't be so emotional" when in fact you have been holding them in. Don't be so emotional means that you should deny your emotions.

> Acknowledging my feelings is kind of scary for me. I get fearful that if I feel sadness, I'm going to withdraw into depression . . . . I fear that I'm going to fall apart. It's getting much better. I'm able to cry more often now and I let myself do that. I'm not falling apart and it is acceptable and all right to feel sad. There is a big difference between feeling sad and feeling sorry for myself.
>
> Agnes

One of your main reasons for denying your emotions is related to your fear about what might happen if you let them out. Ask yourself, "What is the worst thing that could happen if I release my emotions?" Whatever your answer is, that is your worst fear. Chances are releasing your emotions will be a positive experience for you. You will not only be releasing your emotions, but finding parts of yourself that have been denied. They are your emotions, express them, do what you want with them. Exchange your control and fear for release and growth.

Approval Needs

_____ I constantly seek approval and affirmation.
_____ I am extremely loyal even in the face of evidence that the loyalty is undeserved.
_____ I lie when it would be just as easy to tell the truth.

When we constantly want approval from others, we may be loyal to them even when they don't deserve it. We often tell them what we think they want to hear, even if this means that we are lying. It is almost as if we are saying that any relationship is better than no relationship. If you want others' approval, what does *their* approval mean to *you?* Have you ever asked yourself why their approval is so important to you?

Many adult daughters felt that getting approval from others was related to their own self-esteem. It was a way by which they could feel that they were doing the right thing and that they were accepted. The lower your self-esteem, the more you may rely on others to provide external validation of your worth as a person.

> That was very frightening because I never knew what feelings I had because I avoided them. I had buried them and pushed them aside to please other people and to get other people's approval. As a result there was a lot of pain that I had to go through and I'm still experiencing it.
>
> Margaret

A dilemma for most adult daughters, however, was that many of the people whose approval they wanted were not the healthiest people in their lives.

For example, adult daughters shared that they often wanted the approval of the alcoholic parent, or from their adult relationship person even though they knew that the alcoholic or their relationship person caused them much pain. It is as if you want approval from someone whose behavior you do not approve of! Now that's a mixed message if I ever heard one. We must be able to break free of the "approval trap." (Assuming that it's all right with you. Do you approve?)

Rigidity

_____ I lock myself into a course of action without serious consideration to alternate choices or consequences.

_____ I seek tension and crisis and then complain.

_____ I avoid conflict or aggravate it, but rarely deal with it.

When things go wrong, do you find the best solution or do you accept the first solution? Do you apply the same strategies for handling all problems? Many adult daughters believed they inherited the same problem-solving skills that were used in their families while growing up. If so, this locks you into a pattern of rigidity that is difficult to break.

For example, how good are you in a crisis? It was not uncommon for many adult daughters to state that they were more comfortable in a crisis than they were in everyday living situations. Could it be that you have become accustomed to living on the emotional edge? When you find yourself in "normal" situations, do you find yourself waiting for something to go wrong? Additionally, if something does go wrong, do you find yourself unable to stop discussing it? If so, you may be locked into very rigid patterns and not know it. This may not sound unusual to you because you are probably doing what you know best and what you are most comfortable doing.

For example, being raised in a dysfunctional family means that having things go wrong becomes normal. Later when you are in a truly normal situation, you keep waiting for something negative to occur. Adult daughters often stated that they had to learn new behaviors and break old negative patterns in order to feel comfortable and good about healthy situations and people.

Fear Of Failure

_____ I fear rejection and abandonment, yet I reject others.

_____ I fear failure, but I downgrade my successes.

_____ I fear criticism and judgment, yet I criticize others.

I was always looking for that fatal flaw. I always suspected
that there was something they needed from me and that they
didn't really want me. . . . And eventually it would fizzle. I've
been married and divorced and I've had other relationships
that just haven't worked.

Nora

It is obvious that many of these characteristics are two
sided. That is, you do one thing while simultaneously
doing another. What about you, do you have any of the
above fears but undermine your own successes or do you
do the same thing to other people that you fear being done
to you? Many of the adult daughters who did, stated that
one of the reasons for their behaviors was that they were
unsure of themselves.

A characteristic that is not on this list, but was shared
by many adult daughters was that they had problems
making their own decisions. How good are you at making
decisions on your own or do you ask everyone else what
you should do? Were you criticized as a child when you
made your own decisions, or were your decisions considered to be poor choices?

If you fear failure, is it based solely on being afraid to
fail or is it based on a fear that others will reject or
abandon you if you fail? Another aspect of the fear of
failure is related to a fear of criticism. How well do you
handle criticism? If you are criticized, do you take it so
personally that you emotionally fall apart? If you are
criticized, do you feel that not only are you rejected by
whoever criticizes you, but also that you reject yourself?

Well, how did you do on the above questions? Did you
identify with all of them or only a few? If you identified
strongly with many of the questions and found yourself
frequently saying, "I do that," you are not very different
from other adult daughters. In fact, adult daughters
identified overall with the above characteristics 20%
more than did women raised in non-alcoholic families.
Additionally, I found that adult daughters had higher

scores on every one of the characteristics than did women from non-alcoholic families. In other words, when you compare adult daughters to women from non-alcoholic families you will see that on every question adult daughters had higher average scores. (A more detailed table comparing characteristics of adult daughters is in the Appendix. You thought I wasn't going to tell you, didn't you? I had to, after reading these characteristics, how could I be so controlling?)

If you scored highly with the above characteristics does this mean that something is wrong with you? No. It can mean several things. One, you may be very aware and honest about your behaviors. Second, as the daughter of an alcoholic you are very "normal" when compared to other adult daughters. Isn't it comforting to know that you belong and that you are not the only one? Third, you may be out of balance, not a dysfunctional person.

For example, the most commonly identified characteristic of adult daughters was taking yourself very seriously. Do you know what characteristic women raised in non-alcoholic families identified as their most common characteristic? You guessed it, taking themselves very seriously. However, the difference between you and a woman from a non-alcoholic family may not be taking yourself seriously, but rather the degree to which you possess the characteristic. After all, a certain amount of seriousness is found in all adults. It is part of being an adult. Therefore, you don't have to become the opposite of what you are now. You can, however, recover to a point that will allow you to achieve a balance in yourself.

Have you noticed that one of the most common things about the above characteristics is that they are so externally focused? For example, for every characteristic that we identify with, we look outside of ourselves for the answer or we are admitting how much we are externally controlled. The more that you identify with the characteristics, the more you are identifying with others and the less you identify with yourself. Being externally focused is being out of balance. Focusing on yourself and reducing your excessive dependence on others will allow you to not only reduce the above characteristics in you, but also to achieve a sense of personal balance.

8

What Kind Of
Adult Daughter Are You?

Yeah, you still hear the tapes, the old tapes rolling in your head and it's real uncomfortable. Because you know deep down inside you don't want to live your life like that.

Marcia

What kind of adult daughter are you today? Have you carried any childhood patterns into your adulthood? If so, do these patterns help or hinder you now? As a child, you probably adjusted to your situation as best you could. Adapting to life with an alcoholic requires developing certain behaviors to adjust to the situation. Do you know what your adjustment behaviors were? Can you identify them or did they "just happen?" For most adult daughters there was no great design to how they adjusted to their alcoholic family, but rather they utilized certain behaviors and personality characteristics in order to minimize pain and to survive their families.

As a child in your family did you ever consider whether your adaptive behaviors were positive or negative for you? Probably not. However, if you could look outside of yourself and examine your in-home "coping strategies" as a child, you would probably assume that your behavior patterns were positive at the time. In other words, they helped you to adjust to the alcoholism in your family. This was not unusual for most adult daughters as children. In fact, according to Susan Volchok, your behavior patterns probably provided guidelines for you and helped you in several ways (Volchok, 1985). For example:

- They kept you from being abandoned.
- They provided you with guidelines for acceptable behavior.
- They met the expectations of others.
- They helped you to create some balance in your life.
- They helped you to overcome inconsistency and chaos.

However, now that you are an adult, do you still use the same patterns when you interact with others, even though you are no longer in the same situation? If so, you have carried your childhood behaviors into your adulthood. Are these behaviors still positive for you? Probably not.

The negative side of continuing to fulfill your patterns according to Susan Volchok are:

- They keep you from being totally yourself.
- They impede you from developing alternative behaviors.
- They affect your self-concept.
- They create pressure for you to comply to old patterns.

Your patterns are not limited to being totally negative or totally positive, but rather they are more likely to be both. For example, you probably have behaviors that you learned in your family that still help you adjust, survive and relate to others today. Although you may have learned these skills painfully, or because you had no choice, they can still work for your benefit.

On the other hand, many of your behaviors that helped you in a crisis are no longer needed when you are not in a crisis. If you continue to use them, they become negative or create new crises for you in your relationships now.

For example, being overly in control might have helped in the alcoholic family, but it sure will cause problems in your current normal relationships.

Most of your patterns were developed over time during your childhood. If you continue to use them, you continue to reinforce them. They are no longer necessary when you leave your crisis, but they are now old patterns and habits. Can you break your old patterns or are you locked into an emotional "habit cage?" Do you feel that because you once developed certain behaviors, you will always have them or do you believe that you can change? More importantly, do you want to break free of childhood behaviors or roles? If they are holding you back and they keep you from growing, you know they are not the patterns necessary to create a healthy you. Will you change your patterns is one question, but are you even aware of them in yourself is another.

Types Of Adult Daughters

I have observed at least eight different patterns of behaviors in adult daughters that have been carried over from their childhoods. I believe that these different patterns will help you to discover and understand yourself more fully. It is one thing to want to change, it is another to know *what* you want to change. How well do you know yourself and your behaviors? Before we discuss each pattern and its characteristics there are several things you should keep in mind as you read.

• **Each type has positive and negative implications.**

You are a survivor and therefore you have had the skills to survive. You possess many positive qualities whether you are aware of them or not. You possess many characteristics that have the potential to be positively used. On the other hand, there are characteristics in each type that can cause you pain and keep you from enjoying your life. For each type of adult daughter we will identify positive and negative characteristics. The key to recovery is overcoming the negative characteristics in yourself and turning them into assets. Do you have the key? I am sure that some of you are saying, "The key? I'm not sure I can even find the lock."

- **There are overlaps between the types.**

No one type completely describes an adult daughter. You are more likely to identify with one or several of the types more than with others. You will probably identify with some of the parts of each type. However, most adult daughters are astute at recognizing their behaviors and which type of behaviors apply to them.

- **Not all behaviors can be "alcoholized."**

Not all of your characteristics can be traced to being a daughter of an alcoholic. You know that other factors contribute to who you are. One of these, for example, can be your birth order in your family. It is commonly agreed that certain personality characteristics are found in children, depending upon their ordinal position in their families. For example, if you are the oldest or the firstborn, you supposedly possess such characteristics as being self-assured, a responsible high achiever, need recognition from others, focus on semantics and respond to problems analytically.

If you are the second child, some of your characteristics might be that you feel insecure until you know where you fit, that you can detect the emotional needs of others, you listen well and you can become emotionally distant.

Third-born children are usually comfortable with people, possess good social skills, develop in-depth relationships slowly, find it difficult to separate from relationships and withdraw during conflict until they find a solution.

The fourth child in a family is usually outgoing, adventuresome, less ambitious, makes friends easily, takes on the stress of others to relieve tension in a relationship, impulsive and demonstrative when dealing with feelings.

In order to keep from getting too many letters from those of you who are fifth, sixth or higher position daughters, researchers indicate that the characteristics begin to repeat themselves beginning with the fifth child. Thus the fifth child would have the characteristics of the first and the sixth child would have those of the second, and so on (Hoopes, 1989).

As we examine each type of adult daughter, we will be discussing how patterns were developed in her alcoholic family. You, however, will be able to add to your understanding of each type by considering how your birth order may have influenced how you adjusted. When we account for birth order and gender development, I believe we will find some of the same characteristics that we find among adult daughters and in women from the healthiest of families. Not everything can be attributed to alcoholism.

• **Patterns can be changed.**

Your patterns and characteristics can be changed, altered or abandoned. For each type we will discuss the transitions needed to change what may be liabilities into assets.

Are you ready to find yourself? Let's begin. This is kind of like reading your horoscope, isn't it? Your horoscope, however, supposedly tells you what is ahead. Your typology is supposedly based on where you have been and thus talks about your past and how it has contributed to who you are today. Therefore, your typology should have nothing to do with predicting your future. Without change, however, it will predict it perfectly.

The Achiever

Ladies and gentlemen, presenting the all-knowing, ever competent, totally in control, most responsible woman in the world and perfect adult daughter. Does this sound like your introduction to the world? It looks good to others, doesn't it? How does it look to you?

The achieving adult daughter is very accomplishment-oriented. If this is you, you know the pattern very well. It is through your accomplishments that you are recognized. You believe that if your behavior is worth something, then you are worth something. The problem with this kind of thinking is that your worth is always external. Other people hold your validation and the only way to get it is to do things that they recognize as worthwhile.

Usually getting some validation is not a problem for you because you are extremely competent and skilled. If you have problems, it is because you realize that you cannot validate yourself internally. The emotional motivation behind most achieving adult daughters is a sense of inadequacy, of not being good enough. How many times have we heard from adult daughters that whatever they did, it was not good enough? How did they respond to this? They tried harder. Not being good enough can also mean that you feel you are not as good as other people. Deep down inside you feel that others are always better than you and you are constantly trying to prove yourself. To whom — them or you?

As you might suspect, perfectionism is a classic characteristic of the achiever. For example, if you think that something is okay or done correctly, does it have to be 100% correct? On the other hand, does it only take 1% error for the entire thing to be wrong?

> I'm my own worst enemy when it comes to beating myself up. I can do it without any help from anybody. If I had done it this way instead of the way I did, it would have been better. But I did it this way and I made a mistake, I got caught and the whole world is going to fall in on top of me because I made a mistake. So I try hard not to make mistakes in my job, my home or in relationships.
>
> Mary Carol

In relationships, the achiever wants to be in control and is usually willing to do more than her share to get it. If you are an achiever, do you usually intellectualize rather than express your feelings? Do you have an image of what a "perfect relationship" should be, but rarely find one to live up to your expectations? When there are problems in your relationship, rather than dealing with it, you will do what you do best, such as work harder at your job. This keeps you externally focused. You keep people at an emotional distance and rarely have your needs met as a result of keeping others away. All of these behaviors allow you to feel in control and safe. However, do they allow you to have the kind of relationships that you would like?

Adult daughter achievers have so much going for them because of their skills and competencies. With a little adjustment and the development of the ability to validate themselves internally for being a healthy person as opposed to for what they do, they can recover very well. And remember, recovering well does not mean recovering perfectly.

The potential positive and leftover negative patterns of the achiever are:

Positive	Negative
Competent	Overly competitive
Good in a crisis	Perfectionist
Reliable	Difficulty relaxing
Meets goals	Fails to take care of self
Powerful and in control	Can't express feelings
Successful	Externally validated only
Survivor	Workaholic
Motivates self and others	Never wrong
	Marries a dependent person
	Compulsive
	Fears failure
	Unable to play

Transitions needed for the Adult Daughter Achiever

- Develop an internal sense of validation in yourself.
- Learn to say no to others and yourself.
- Find time for yourself.
- Learn to relax, slow down.
- Learn to appreciate yourself.

The Triangulator

The adult daughter who is a triangulator never deals with anyone or anything directly. If you do this, chances are when something goes wrong for you, you are more likely to find an outside reason or excuse rather than look at yourself.

For example, you get into trouble and blame it on the weather. You might be having a problem in a relationship, but rather than deal with it directly, you put it off because you fear it might upset someone else. Most triangulators are typically noticed when they get into trouble, display conduct disorders or develop relationship problems but will not focus on any issue directly.

Adult daughter triangulators probably learned their behaviors from their parents' relationship. The adult daughter may have been used as the focal point between the parents because they did not want to deal directly with each other. Therefore, they used their daughter as an excuse or an external focus point not to deal with their own problems. Did this happen to you and are you repeating the pattern?

> Fifteen years ago I was blaming my mother for ruining my life. I would have never married that jerk if it weren't for her getting divorced, marrying my stepdad and making my life so miserable that I had to move out. I blamed her for that and I was very angry with her.
>
> Gloria

Often the emotional motivation behind triangulating is anger, resentment, hurt and a fear of abandonment. These emotions often lead the adult daughter into inappropriate behaviors for which she is now held responsible, but which she would like to blame on others.

The triangulator is closely associated to Lee Ann Hoff's idea that some people in a crisis react by channeling their emotions into negative behaviors.

> As a kid I could be real angry and I would be sent to my room. I would sit there and smolder and just be angry. Now I'm trying to learn what's beneath the anger and work through it. Generally, it's fear and loneliness. It's fear of rejection, fear of abandonmment or fear of being hurt.
>
> Adele

Very few adult daughters fall into this pattern. But for those of you who do, you are likely to have certain relationship problems.

For example, if you have relationship problems do you deal with them or blame the other person? Do you find yourself always manipulating to get what you want? Has your relationship partner accused you of being irresponsible and not contributing your share to the relationship? Do you find it difficult to be close to someone because you believe that no one understands you? Both positive and negative characteristics could emerge from this pattern once the negative behaviors are overcome.

Positive	Negative
Creative	Conducts disorders
Courage	Poor communication skills
Good under pressure	Blames world for problems
Lots of friends	Manipulative
Commands attention	Angry
Adventuresome	Irresponsible
	Substance abuser
	Passive-aggressive

Transitions needed for the Adult Daughter Triangulator

- Learn to accept responsibility for your behaviors.
- Learn appropriate ways to handle or release anger.
- Learn how to communicate directly.
- Learn alternative ways to handle stress.

The Passive One

If you are a passive adult daughter, your patterns are very difficult to assess. Unlike some of the other patterns, it is not what you are doing that makes you noticed, but rather what you are not doing. Adult daughters who display some of the other typologies can be defined by their actions and what they are doing. Passive adult daughters can be recognized by what is being done to them or how they usually just go along with everything. They are never a player in the game, but always a spectator. They are never actors, but reactors. Their unspoken motto of passivity implies that "life is a rehearsal."

Does any of this describe you? Do you have a low opinion of yourself or feel that your needs are not as important as others? Do you go along to get along too often? Do you often feel that if others knew all about you, they wouldn't like you? If so, you have some of the passive adult daughter characteristics. Your emotional motivations as a passive adult daughter are: you feel unimportant, what you want doesn't count and you usually feel hopeless in a crisis.

> With low self-esteem, I constantly cast myself in the master-servant relationship role. Giving, giving, giving until you have nothing left for your own development and growth. I only felt satisfaction when everyone else around me was happy and content. I completely suffocated my own needs and feelings . . . the voice of denial nags at me saying, "Your life is full of opportunities, it's not that bad." I had no identity and therefore became an appendage of my husband.
>
> Jeannie

In relationships passive adult daughters are likely to tolerate a tremendous amount of inappropriate behaviors, are always willing to be second and seldom express their needs. If conflicts develop, they are likely to take the path of least resistance, which usually means, do what the other person wants. Passive adult daughters internalize relationship problems, but will not discuss them for fear of abandonment. Additionally, they are at risk for developing eating disorders.

Passive adult daughter characteristics include:

Positive	Negative
Tolerant	Doesn't stand up for self
Willing to help others	Low self-worth
Highly adaptable	Always puts others first
Loyal friends	Lonely
Independent	Fears reality
Good listener	Depressed
Empathic	Joyless
	Used in relationships
	Eating disorders
	Confused
	Shy

Transitions needed for Passive Adult Daughters

- Learn to take care of yourself first.
- Do things to raise your self-esteem.
- Learn to feel good about yourself.
- Learn to accept being liked by others.
- Stop doing what you do not do; take action.

The Other-Directed One

Adult daughters, who are other directed, rely heavily on others' opinions of what they should do, hide their feelings by displaying the exact opposite of their emotions and feel as if their lives are out of control. If you are an other-directed adult daughter, do you believe that you must portray the exact opposite of how you feel? Why would you do this? Usually it is because you feel that if you do not, you will be rejected or abandoned by others. The emotional motivation for allowing yourself to be other directed is deeply rooted in a fear of exposure of your feelings and your needs. It is a fear of being abandoned.

I found that I grew up with a fear that my father was going to leave. It was a fear of abandonment and losing somebody important. I realized that I brought my fear into my marriage. It's like from the day we got married, subconsciously thinking, I know he's going to leave me. He's not going to love me enough to stay. I started building up defenses and at the same time trying to do everything he wanted to keep him from leaving. So far, he's still here.

Denise

The adult daughter who is other-directed believes that to be accepted, she should do what others want her to do. If she is in pain, she will hide it because she believes that it is unacceptable to others. Usually you will hide your pain by displaying the exact opposite of how you feel. After all, if you pretend that you are happy, no one will notice your turmoil, or so you believe.

Do you often feel as if you are "programmed?" For example, do you feel that you must constantly meet everyone else's expectations, but never your own? When you are other-directed you become externally focused. You often say to yourself, "I feel like I do everything for everyone else, but I never do anything for myself."

Other-directed adult daughters have a limited sense of self-identity and identity boundary problems. For example, they are not sure where their identity ends and another person's begins because they overly identify with what the other person thinks they should do. The other-directed adult daughter looks into the mirror and sees a reflection of herself not as she sees it, but how she believes other people see her.

If you are an other-directed adult daughter how do you respond in relationships? Do you have difficulty making decisions in a relationship? Do you constantly defer to the other person by saying, "Whatever you want, I want?" Do you feel that in your relationships you are behaviorally stuck? In other words, you cannot behave the way you would like and you are limited to only those behaviors of which your partner approves. Additionally, in your relationships you are probably overly sensitive to criticism, deny your own feelings and have difficulty establishing your boundaries.

The positive and negative characteristics of the other-directed adult daughter include:

Positive	Negative
Attracts attention	Overly controlled by others
Charming	Tense, anxious
Sense of humor	Over-reactive
Can anticipate needs	Shallow relationships
Adaptable	Indecisive
Team player	No sense of self
Cooperative	Overly dependent
Joyful	Needs to please others only
Energetic	Needs constant approval
	Poor sense of boundaries

Transitions needed for Other-Directed Adult Daughters

- Learn to develop a sense of what is right for you.
- Stop being controlled by others.
- Learn to express your needs and ideas.
- Establish your own sense of self and boundaries.
- Start doing what you want to do.

Conflict Avoider

I tend to be a people-pleaser, a "Red Crosser." I look for people I can help and rescue. I used to thrive on chaos and challenges, but I am learning to love calmness, order and quietness in my life. Learning to love myself is a very big problem. I had to learn to get my hands off everything in the lives of my husband and children.

Stephanie

Do you find yourself in the middle of everyone else's problems? Are you willing to help everyone else with their problems, but avoid your own? If so, you may be a conflict-avoider adult daughter. This type of adult daughter appears to be very willing to help others. She is the neighborhood counselor and the person who others will rely on for solutions. The irony is that this adult daughter wants to avoid conflicts in her life more than anything else. Why does she help other people with their problems then? Because they are *other* people's problems, thus she can avoid facing her own.

For example, the more I would be willing to help you and my cousins and my neighbors, the more I can keep you away from me and the less I have to face my own problems.

The emotional motivation for the conflict avoider is a fear of arguments and personal conflict. She will do anything to avoid an argument, whether hers or someone else's. If this describes you, it is likely that you engage in a lot of people-pleasing behaviors. The conflict avoider does not think that there is any such thing as a healthy argument. All arguments are to be avoided. However, she can spot trouble before it occurs because she is very sensitive to the warning signs.

How does she respond when she sees trouble coming? She gets out her box of emotional Band-Aids and applies them before the wounds get too deep. However, this approach usually leads to postponing problems, denying the real issues involved and never having anything resolved.

In relationships the conflict-avoider adult daughter is highly vulnerable to being used. She will disproportionately focus on the problems of the other person and will do almost anything to keep arguments from occurring in her relationships. Ironically, she hates arguments, but when they occur, she feels it is her responsibility to resolve them.

How does she resolve them? By minimizing their existence, denial or avoiding the necessary steps involved for resolution. In her relationships she often feels that she is constantly placating others and usually has low self-worth. She suffers from a "justifiable negative attention" image of herself.

For example, she believes that the only time she can receive emotional support from others is when something has happened to her beyond her control such as an accident or an illness. Then it is okay to receive attention. This puts her at great risk for having to manipulate others in order to get what she wants or needs. She does not feel good about herself thus has difficulty accepting good feelings from others.

Some of the positive and negative characteristics of the conflict avoider are:

Positive	Negative
Willing to help others	Unrealistic opinion of
Good in a crisis	arguments
Good negotiator	Constantly placating others
Problem solver	Powerlessness
Persistent	Depression
Sensitive to others	Denial
Thinks of alternatives	Takes on too many
Good communicator	problems
	Seldom happy
	Intimidated
	Inability to receive
	User relationships

Transitions needed for Conflict-Avoider Adult Daughters

- Recognize and focus on your own problems.
- Quit taking on the problems of others.
- Learn to accept positive attention.
- Learn the difference between helping someone and feeling responsible for their problems and solutions.
- Be willing to receive help from others.

The Hypermature

Do you take yourself very seriously? Are you always emotionally on guard? Do you find it difficult to let yourself go or genuinely to have fun? Have you always felt you were more mature than your peers? If so, chances are you identify very strongly with the hypermature adult daughter pattern.

> I took my role too seriously. I tried too hard to keep my sons away from drugs and alcohol. I was an either/or person with no room for grey areas. I tried to make my children achieve too much and grow up too soon. I loved them through their accomplishments and lived vicariously through their lives. I centered all of my energies around my children and ignored my husband.
>
> Cleo

Hypermaturity is different from the other patterns because it is more indicative of your attitudes than your behaviors. Most of the other patterns focus on the various behavioral patterns. The hypermature adult daughter, however, thinks of herself differently and is very reserved, striving to maintain total control over her emotions. The emotional motivation for hypermaturity is needing to be emotionally on guard and always being prepared.

If you are a hypermature adult daughter, not only do you take yourself very seriously, but you take everything you do seriously. You are the "eternal parent" in the group. You are the one who always thinks of everything that could go wrong, then plan accordingly. Your ability to anticipate actions in other people is almost scary. You are reliable, but have a great deal of difficulty allowing anyone to do anything for you, believing they could not do it as well as you. You also get irritated by people who do not take things as seriously as you do.

Some of the most common problems that we find in hypermature adult daughters is that they have a general feeling of being "burned-out," that something is missing in their lives. Usually they began their lives as adults too early.

For example, they took on tremendous responsibilities in early adolescence, now the emotional overload is beginning to catch up with them. On the other hand they never had time to be a child.

"When I was young, I was never a child," is a common statement by the hypermature adult daughter. It is no wonder they have a difficult time acting their age, even as adults. After all, no one said that we cannot have joy and laughter in our lives now, or that the joy of being a child must be limited to childhood years.

The healthiest people are "age androgynous."

That is, they possess the best aspects of being young and an adult at the same time. One of the best indicators of recovery is developing a healthy sense of humor. The hypermature adult daughter often confuses intellectual sarcasm with humor. Laughter, warmth and time for yourself should be part of every stage of your life, so remember to act your age.

If you are a hypermature adult daughter, how does this affect your relationships? Typically, you are extreme in most of the things you do, including your relationships. You find it difficult to take relationships lightly and make everything too intense. You often hear from your relationship person that you are too serious, "Lighten up, will you." You will feel that you are disproportionately responsible for the success of the relationship. If the relationship fails, you will judge yourself without mercy. Having fun is often missing and even when you do take time for yourself, you are constantly worrying about all the things you have to do. Most of the time you are at risk for feeling overwhelmed in your relationships and emotionally drained.

If the hypermature adult daughter can learn to take it easy and not take everything so seriously, she can change her negative characteristics into assets. The positive and negative characteristics for the hypermature adult daughter include:

Positive	Negative
Organized	Too serious
Analytical	Difficulty expressing
Prepared	emotions
Mature	Constantly needing control

Reliable	Stress-related illnesses
Intuitive	Not much fun
Meets goals	Fearful
Attentive	Driven
	Avoids taking risks
	Critical
	Blames self too much

Transitions needed for the Hypermature Adult Daughter

• Learn to relax and have fun.
• Let others take charge.
• Allow yourself to express emotions.
• Adjust your priorities to reduce feeling overwhelmed.
• Laugh more.

Detacher

The adult daughter who is a detacher wants to remove herself emotionally and psychologically from all situations she feels are undesirable.

This pattern usually starts when you are an adolescent and you decide that although you must live with your dysfunctional family, "It isn't going to bother me anymore." You tried to detach emotionally from the situation and as soon as you were able to leave physically, you were gone. Your assumption was, "All I have to do is leave and I will leave all of this behind."

Knowing when to detach yourself from an unhealthy situation can be a healthy response. The kind of detachment that can cause problems for you is based on what is called *premature closure*. Premature closure occurs when you are not willing to deal with anything or anyone who makes you uncomfortable and your first response is to leave. This does not allow you the opportunity to work things out or find solutions. You use the same response to all problem situations — you leave. The emotional motivation for the adult-daughter detacher is to avoid being hurt. She will attempt this by trying to become non-feeling or emotionally numb.

Do you pretend nothing bothers you? Do you believe you can emotionally separate yourself from situations you don't like? Do you look for solutions in your relationships or the first time something goes wrong, do you want to end it? Do you deny unpleasant events? If so, you might be detaching and not allowing yourself the opportunity for resolution or expressing your feelings. After all, when you detach, you believe you can emotionally detach as well. This is where the problem lies for most detaching adult daughters.

For example, they believe they have successfully detached from their alcoholic family, but don't bring it up! If it didn't affect you emotionally, why such strong emotions about bringing it up? The truth is that most detachers do not detach, but use this pattern as a way of not dealing with the emotional baggage they want to deny. This kind of thinking and behavior puts you in an emotional trap. If you detached successfully, there would be no emotions from your past, but if the feelings persist, does that mean that you weren't successful?

As you might suspect if you are a detaching adult daughter, you will be very hard to reach. You believe that by detaching you have protected yourself. You believe that if you don't detach, you will be vulnerable and not in control of your emotions. Therefore, in order to work on your issues, you will need to accept that some things have affected you and your emotions have not been resolved. You will need to confront a very intimidated person — yourself.

In relationships the adult daughter detacher wants to flee immediately if everything is not comfortable. If she even senses that trouble is coming, she is likely to want out. On the other hand, her perception of what constitutes a healthy relationship is not realistic. To her a good relationship is one that is totally trouble-free. It is unlikely she will find one so will jump from relationship to relationship, either looking for the good one, or leaving the existing one early because she senses problems coming.

Always detaching has denied her the skills to resolve relationship conflict. Her opinion of relationship problems is that they are caused by the other person.

For example, she has had six relationships with men. All six relationships collapsed. What does she deduce from her experiences? There is something wrong with men and the same thing is wrong with each one of them. Now in her seventh relationship the same problems arise again. How does she respond? By telling him, "Look if you're having problems with this relationship, they are your problems. If you can't handle it, I'm out of here." I know what you are thinking, you've waited years to tell that to some guy. Sounds pretty good to you, but look what the detacher has denied herself. She denies herself developing the kinds of skills that will help in relationships. She denies her own feelings and she denies developing a healthy concept of what makes a good relationship. She becomes detached from her own needs.

> My biggest problem was disliking myself. I never believed others really liked or loved me and I was always suspicious of their motives. I have a fear of anger in myself and in others. I lack trust. I always have a wall between myself and others to assure that I don't get hurt.
>
> Grace

The positive and negative characteristics of the adult daughter detacher include . . .

Positive	Negative
Perceptive	Rigid attitudes
Sets limits	Jealous, suspicious
Can spot trouble	Defiant
Independent	Lonely
Self-motivated	Non-feeling
Traveler	High risk for addiction
Nonconformist	Secretive
	Inner anger
	Fears being hurt
	Denial

Transitions needed for Adult-Daughter Detachers

- Learn interpersonal relationship skills.
- Develop a realistic concept of healthy relationships.
- Develop alternatives for handling stress.
- Learn to identify and express your emotions.
- Learn to accept help and support from others.

The Invulnerable

Is there such a thing as a healthy adult daughter? Absolutely! She is known as the invulnerable adult daughter. There are many studies that have found that some children who are raised in extremely dysfunctional families emerge as very healthy adults (Garmezy, 1976; Werner, 1986).

I could never understand how adult children were consistently described in only negative terms. I was always wondering where do the healthy ones belong or what about the healthy parts that are found in all adult children? I believe that it is possible for the invulnerable pattern to develop in adult daughters in three ways.

One way is when the adult daughter, without any formal intervention, emerges as a very healthy adult.

The second form occurs when the adult daughter is able to work through many of her issues and feelings. Through her personal recovery she becomes an invulnerable.

The third way occurs when you begin to recognize and accept that parts of you are healthy and competent. Parts of you are invulnerable. Why did we identify positive characteristics in each of the previous seven patterns? Because parts of you are very positive. More importantly, you have the abilities to grow even further.

What do I mean by invulnerable? Do I mean that nothing affects you and that you are indestructible? No. The true invulnerable adult daughter is one who does not deny her feelings, her experiences or her pain. When she is feeling vulnerable, she will not only admit it, but will ask for and accept help. Many of the other typologies will deny their feelings when they need help, thus deny help.

The invulnerable adult daughter does not deny, but accepts then acts to maintain her own health.

How well do you take care of your emotional self? Are you willing to allow yourself to admit when you are vulnerable? Do you ever ask for help and allow yourself to receive it? Can you identify your invulnerable traits? Are you turning your childhood liabilities into adult characteristics that will work well for you? Invulnerables are made not born. You become invulnerable through your actions and your attitudes. You learn to use the positive traits that have been identified in all adult daughters. You learn that you have never lost your abilities to hope, to risk, to try, to forgive, to grow beyond your injuries, to share, to love and recognize that you are a good person.

In relationships invulnerable adult daughters know how to achieve balance. If you are an invulnerable adult daughter, your relationships are healthy. You know how to give and receive. Your emotional and physical needs are being met. You are able to express your needs and able to negotiate openly with your partner. You can be yourself without fearing rejection and you are loved for who you are. You are also a great person to be in a relationship with. Your health is obvious and contagious.

Since the invulnerable is very different from the other patterns, I will identify some characteristics found in invulnerable adult daughters. I will not identify needed transitions because the invulnerable adult daughter is always growing.

How many of the following invulnerable behaviors do you have?

- You know how to attract and use the support of those who are around you.
- You have developed a healthy sense of humor.
- You have developed a well-balanced sense of autonomy.
- You are socially at ease and others are comfortable around you.
- You are willing to identify and express your feelings.

- You can work through your problems.
- You are neither controlled nor controlling.
- You do not live in fear of your past, but with the joy of the present.
- You like yourself.

Today I love myself. Today I am really special . . . . I see myself like a rose. Better yet, when you plant a garden, you plant a seed. A seed has been planted in me and it's growing into a flower. A flower that's blossoming. As it opens, doors open into my life. For each door that opens, there's a new experience. From that experience I find inner peace and self-love that we all deserve. I sure do. . . . Today I'm okay, I'm really okay.

Lillian

9

I'm Not Co-dependent, Are We?

Do you find yourself using old solutions to new problems and they don't work? Are you torn between your old patterns of behavior and a conscious awareness to want to change, but you don't know how? Do you know what is holding you back and keeping you from growing? Are you afraid to be yourself, especially in relationships? If these questions apply to you, you have many "leftovers" from childhood which lead you into patterns of unhealthy behaviors. These patterns can lead to co-dependency.

> Yeah, you're always looking over your shoulder waiting for the cloud, right?
>
> Melissa

Co-dependency has been defined many ways and its origins can be traced back to assessing how non-alcoholic family members are affected by someone else's alcoholism.

However, it is more than just exposure to alcoholism. It is exposure to life in a dysfunctional family as well. Even co-dependency cannot be totally alcoholized.

For example, Robert Subby defines co-dependency as "an emotional, psychological and behavioral condition that develops as a result of an individual's prolonged exposure to, and practice of, a set of oppressive *rules* — rules which prevent the open expression of feeling, as well as the direct discussion of personal and interpersonal problems" (Subby, 1987).

Did you grow up in a family that was not only alcoholic, but had many spoken and unspoken oppressive rules? No one ever voted on these rules, but they sure were maintained. Did you feel that at times you were living a life in an emotional dictatorship? Do you still feel out of balance as a result of your experiences?

> It's difficult to put values, trust and love back together again because what you thought it was, isn't there anymore. We were raised to be very independent. It's difficult to allow others in to see what is going on inside me . . . it's a difficult life being the independent person, trying to make everything work the way you think it should, and put the pieces back together.
>
> Wendy

In the previous chapter on behavior patterns if you disproportionately identified with the negative characteristics, you probably have many co-dependent behaviors. Co-dependency causes you to be out of balance emotionally and behaviorally in your life. It keeps you externally focused and doesn't allow you to develop a healthy sense of self.

Co-dependency is measured by the degree to which you have been affected by your alcoholic family. When you are out of balance, you are either too much one way or the other.

For example, giving too much in one situation and not enough in another. All adult daughters can display some characteristics that could identify with co-dependency, but it is the degree to which these characteristics exist that determines whether or not they are co-dependent. If many of your behaviors are causing pain for you, and it is obvious that you are stuck in your old patterns, you will probably identify very heavily with the characteristics of co-dependency.

High Risk Characteristics For Co-dependency

Are you a co-dependent? Could you become co-dependent? What are the characteristics and are you at risk for developing them?

How much do you identify with the following statements?

- I have an over/underdeveloped sense of responsibility and it is easier for me to be concerned about others, even if it means ignoring legitimate needs in myself.
- I "stuff" my feelings about my own childhood and have lost the ability to feel or express feelings because it hurts too much.
- I am physically/emotionally isolated and am afraid of people, especially authority figures.
- I have become addicted to approval/excitement and have lost my identity in the process.
- I am frightened by angry people and personal criticism.
- I live as a victim.
- I judge myself harshly and have a low self-esteem.
- I am very dependent and am terrified of abandonment. I will hold onto any relationship to keep from being abandoned.
- I experience guilt feelings when I stand up for myself.
- I have become chemically dependent or a compulsive under/overeater or found another compulsive personality person, such as a workaholic, to fulfill my compulsive needs.

The above characteristics, if displayed too much, would put you at a very high risk for becoming co-dependent. However, when we consider co-dependency, I believe we must be cautious not to label too many behaviors as co-dependent.

For example, you may have noticed that many of the behaviors associated with co-dependency focus on caring, thinking of others, helping in a crisis, needing approval from others and perceiving your life in relationship to others. In and of themselves, what is wrong with these behaviors? Aren't these the kinds of qualities that we would like to have in ourselves and in our friends? The real question becomes, what is the line between being a warm, loving and caring person and being co-dependent? If we go too far in saying that any of your behaviors that support someone else are co-dependent, are we saying that you are wrong to care about another person?

I believe that even co-dependency itself must be assessed from a position of balance. Recently the tendency has been to define co-dependency too vaguely and too broadly which results in almost all nurturing behaviors being included. I have read authors who state that 96% of American families are co-dependent! I suppose this means that if you are co-dependent, you must be normal! What are the other 4% of families? When the definition of co-dependency becomes too vague, we become vulnerable to unjustifiable conviction.

If you want to know whether you suffer from co-dependency or are at a high risk for developing it, you must assess your behaviors and your emotional motivations very honestly. To accept too broad a definition might mean that you believe that you must become so independent, you need absolutely no one or that helping someone is an indicator of how ill you are. Remember the idea is to look for balance, not absolutes. If we become too absolute in our willingness to embrace co-dependency as an explain-all-behaviors phenomenon, I believe we will be co-dependent in our understanding of co-dependency itself.

Co-dependent Relationships

How do you know if you are out of balance in your life? Let's examine how you respond in your relationships as one example of your behaviors that could be vulnerable to co-dependency.

As an adult daughter are you a healthy, warm and loving person or are you co-dependent and trying to hide it by becoming warm and loving for everyone else? One of the best indicators of whether or not you are co-dependent depends upon how much your needs are being met. On the other hand, if you are a very giving person and your needs are still genuinely being met, you are not giving too much and you are not out of balance.

For example, Robin Norwood in her book, *Women Who Love Too Much*, talks about the problem of loving too much, especially by women who were raised in dysfunctional families. However, is the real problem loving too much or not being loved enough? She tells us that many women, who do not feel loved and whose needs are not being met, fall into the trap of trying to give what they hope to get (Norwood, 1985). Thus by giving love away, you hope to get it in return.

What happens to you, however, if you give tremendous amounts away and have very little returned?

If you continue in this pattern of constantly giving more than you get, you are locked into a co-dependent relationship. In a healthy relationship, your needs should be met as well as the other person's needs. In a co-dependent relationship only one person's needs are being met and unfortunately it is at the expense of deferring your needs.

> Without realizing it I wound up picking very needy men. I played the big sister role. I wasn't able to share feelings because I was always looking to be a better person. If I was good enough, then maybe he would be happy. I really recreated the role I played with my father. Naturally, it didn't work.
>
> Maureen

If you are a "good" co-dependent, you are good at meeting other people's needs and lousy at meeting your own. If you want to be healthy and have your needs met, you have to give up being a "good" co-dependent.

Do you engage in any co-dependent behaviors in your relationships? Ask yourself if you identify with the following characteristics of co-dependent relationships.

- I will do almost anything to keep my relationship from falling apart because I don't want to be alone.
- I believe there is no such thing as too much effort or time to help the other person in my relationship.
- I never had much love in any of my relationships, so I don't expect much now.
- I try as hard as I can to please the other person in my relationship all the time. I am intimidated if they get angry.
- I often become a care giver to needy people but have difficulty receiving nurturing from others.
- I keep getting into relationships with people who I think I can change or hoping will change because they love me.
- I usually do more than my share in a relationship and for some reason continue doing it.
- I never feel I am as good as the person with whom I am in a relationship.
- I want to be in control in my relationships, but often find myself being controlled. I react to this by becoming even more controlling.
- If there are problems in my relationships, I still prefer to think of how it could be, rather than how it is.
- I am in love with being "in love."
- I keep getting into relationships with people who are "therapy projects" and usually get emotionally hurt while trying to fix them.
- I get depressed easily in my relationships, especially if everything is not going well.
- I am not sure that I can be comfortable or that I can stay very long in a healthy relationship.

How much you have been affected by your childhood, how many negative patterns you have carried into your adulthood and how successfully you can recover, depends upon how co-dependent you are. One thing about co-dependency is certain. Having it will keep you from recovering and from becoming healthy.

Adult daughters with many problems in their lives are the ones trapped in co-dependency. It can surface in your relationships, your parenting skills, your self-esteem and in your attempts to recover. If you are not sure that you possess any co-dependent characteristics, let's break it down into other behaviors and see how much you identify with them. After all, a "good" co-dependent is not likely to be aware of her behaviors. When you are constantly focused on others, you have little time for your own needs.

Breaking the cycle of co-dependency begins with discovering that you have some of the patterns. Please remember this does not make you a "bad" person or naive for not knowing it. You probably did what made the most sense for you in your childhood. This was called "child-sense" and it helped you to survive. Now the patterns are "nonsense" and they keep you from growing. These patterns no longer fit and cause you pain. To break the patterns, however, you have to know your patterns.

Are you maintaining any of the following patterns?

Progressive Defeat

Do you feel despair or hopelessness about changing yourself or the current situation you are in? Have you exchanged your attitude of hope for one of pessimism? If so, you are developing an attitude of progressive defeat, an indicator of co-dependency. Even when you do well, do you feel good about it or do you still have a low self-esteem?

Living In Fear

Living in fear can happen in many ways for adult daughters. For example, it can occur when you are preoccupied with the problems of others or you are unable to make claims for your own needs. Other symptoms of living in fear include being overly responsible, manipulating others' behaviors, persistent anxiety and the feelings of dread. Do you fear the future? Are you often afraid that things will never get better for you? Do you fear that you are stuck in your life and will never learn how to break the patterns that hold you? These are all signs of living in fear and fear plays a major role in co-dependency.

Impaired Identity

We have talked so often about how your identity can be fragmented from having an alcoholic family. Loss of identity and difficulty in boundary separation from others plays a major part in keeping you co-dependent. When we need others to validate who we are, we suffer from impaired identity development. Not being able to separate from others and to establish your own identity keeps you at a high risk for maintaining co-dependency. When you are co-dependent, your life is never your own, it belongs to someone else. But you may never realize this because you are too busy identifying with them.

Co-dependency is a trap. The core of co-dependency is giving up your own identity. The more co-dependent you are, the more you identify with someone else. The more you identify with them, the less you think of yourself. Unfortunately, whoever you disproportionately identify with will not help you break free. They will selfishly allow you to support them at the expense of sacrificing yourself.

It's time to say, "No more human sacrifices."

Shame

Adult daughters often mentioned shame as a problem, but it took many different forms. For some adult daughters, shame was associated with feeling guilty about not only their own behaviors, but also about others' behaviors. Wanting to deny family problems, especially alcoholism, can be motivated by shame.

Statements of self-hatred such as "I'm no good," "I can't do anything right," "I never please anyone," or "I'm not as good as other people," are examples of how shame can foster the development of co-dependency.

Confusion

Are you often surprised to find out that what you thought was real or normal isn't? Co-dependency can keep you not only separated from yourself, but also separated from reality. After all, once you honestly see a dysfunctional situation for what it is, it becomes harder to deny. Denial keeps you from accepting reality, but it also keeps you confused.

Other symptoms of confusion involve being very gullible (the "I'll-believe-anything" syndrome) and being very indecisive. When we are not sure of what is real, we believe everything we are told. One of the prerequisites to being used is allowing others to control what you believe not only about them, but also about yourself.

Anger

The co-dependent person is often a very angry person, but is not sure at what or who. What do you do with your anger? Do you express it or keep it inside? Do you handle it directly or do you redirect it toward someone or some activity to cover it up? Redirecting your anger is a co-dependent behavior.

Some adult daughters were spiritually angry, feeling that God had let them down, not only in childhood, but also in their adult lives.

Another form of anger is unidentified anger. Do you ever find yourself walking around feeling angry for no apparent reason; you just feel ticked off? This should signal something is wrong. The problem now is finding out what. Anger that is not released or confronted does not dissolve. In fact not only does it stay, but it continues to grow. Co-dependency might redirect your anger, but it sure doesn't get rid of it.

If you identified strongly with at least four of the above patterns you are at risk for co-dependency. Co-dependent adult daughters consistently shared that they felt stuck and did become more aware that co-dependency impedes their recovery. I believe that the greatest consequence of co-dependency is that it keeps you from being yourself.

Me Phobia

Karen Blaker in her book, *Born to Please*, identifies the fear of being yourself as "me phobia" (Blaker, 1988). Do you often feel like an emotional imposter? Are you afraid of revealing the true you? Me phobia keeps you from being yourself and is especially apparent when you feel you cannot be yourself in your relationships. Me phobia makes you feel you must always be on guard to please the other person. Additionally, you are always careful not to let the real you come through. After a while you become an expert at doing both. You become skilled at doing what others want, while simultaneously masking who you are. You become an extension of others at the expense of being separated from yourself.

Another form of me phobia is the fear of getting to know yourself. After all, what if you don't like what you find? Will you change or will you continue to fear yourself?

Do you suffer from me phobia? Read the following signs of me phobia, according to Karen Blaker, and explore your self-diagnosis.

- When you're upset, you hide your feelings rather than risk causing a scene.
- When you have an opinion, you're easily convinced to change your mind.
- You often feel exhausted but keep going anyway.
- You overeat or fail to eat when you are nervous or upset.
- You find it hard to voice your negative feelings, especially, "I'm angry" or "I'm hurt."
- If you have strong emotions about something, either good or bad, your reaction is usually to cry.
- You try to avoid being alone and feel anxious or upset when you're on your own.
- You avoid making decisions, even simple ones, without asking the opinion of others.
- You often act cheerful when you're really sad.

- You believe that you're very good at reading the feelings of other people.
- You are the "rock," the one others depend on to keep things running smoothly.
- There are things you would like to do, but you're putting your plans on hold until a future time when people will need you less.
- You avoid making requests if you think they will inconvenience others.
- You feel guilty when you have to say no to others.

Blaker believes that if you said yes to four or more of the above statements, you have me phobia. She believes you are a prime candidate for always reacting to others, never yourself.

Me phobia and co-dependency were made for each other. They will live co-dependently ever after, but they sure won't live happily ever after. Will you? If you are at a high risk for co-dependency and you want to reduce your risk or alter your behaviors, you must begin with yourself. You need to overcome me phobia. It may not be as difficult as you think.

Throughout this book, we have consistently stressed your positive characteristics as well as negative ones. The same principle applies to co-dependency. Do I think that co-dependency exists? Yes. Do I think that the term can be overused and abused? Yes. As I mentioned earlier, there is a great difference between being a warm and loving person and being co-dependent. The reason that overcoming me phobia may not be so difficult is because there are many parts of you, perhaps undiscovered, that have the potential to make you a very healthy person.

If taken to an extreme, what is the cure for co-dependency? Is it to display the exact opposite of all of the indicative behaviors? What does that mean?

For example, does it mean that you give up being emotional, being able to feel, being able to empathize with others, caring about other people or being compassionate? I wonder if the concept of co-dependency is not "male dominated" in thinking. That is, it often appears that to overcome co-dependency, you are asked to give up behaviors and characteristics that are traditionally identified more with women than men.

Co-dependency means being out of balance. Overcoming it does not mean giving up your potentially best qualities. Although it appears true that many of the characteristics of co-dependency have been directed towards women, is it because women are more at risk for these behaviors? Or is it because women have been more willing to identify and admit when they are out of balance? It is also possible we have not discovered what male co-dependent behaviors are.

For example, have you ever considered that there can be female and male forms of co-dependency? Adult daughter forms of co-dependency can develop from identifying *too* much with other people. Adult son forms of co-dependency can develop from identifying *too* little with other people. Therefore, it is ridiculous to ask adult daughters to give up their gender behaviors, which might be mistaken for co-dependency, in order to recover.

If you are afraid to use your best qualities, you are still suffering from me phobia. Do not give up your qualities of being emotional, compassionate, empathetic, sensitive, intimate and loving. Don't risk missing the emotional boat. At least half the males I know miss the emotional boat every day. They wouldn't know a healthy relationship if they fell into one.

Use your emotional qualities to help yourself first. Pull them back when you have given them too freely to others and give them to yourself.

If you give everything and feel used, you are co-dependent. If you think that you have stopped being co-dependent because you have totally abandoned all giving and emotional behaviors, you are now denying yourself your own health. Either way, the best of you is kept from you. Give yourself a warm loving present. Unwrap who you are, throw the wrapping away and keep the present.

PART THREE

Save You, Save Me

10

Relationships
Or You Married A What?

I have no idea what a healthy relationship is — what marriage is as far as my roles, responsibilities and rights go. I give myself mixed messages. I go after someone who will take care of me, but who is emotionally unavailable. I have love-fear feelings towards sex. I am afraid of men in general. I have feelings of guilt if I follow my interests which differ from my partner.

Marilyn

Are you in a relationship with a "therapy project" or did you marry one? Are you fighting for control of your relationship or are you fighting to get out from under someone else's control of you? Do you feel that something is missing in your relationships, but you are not sure what? On the other hand, are you in a relatively healthy relationship, but you keep waiting for it to fail or to be

129

abandoned? Do you believe that you deserve a healthy relationship or do you feel that you are in the relationship that you deserve?

If you question your relationships and feel uncertain about them, you are like many adult daughters who said one of the major problems today was their relationships. In fact, relationship problems were the most frequently cited concerns for adult daughters.

Before we proceed with relationship problems, let's start with your expectations.

What Do You Want From A Relationship?

Have you ever honestly asked yourself what you want from a relationship? Get a piece of paper, sit down and write on the top of the page, "These are my expectations and wants in a relationship." Now list what you want from a relationship.

How long is your list? How aware are you of what you want? Are there differences between what you want and what you expect? The greater the differences, the more likely you are to be disappointed in your relationships. Many adult daughters recognized great differences in their relationships between what they wanted and what they got, but were still willing to assume most of the blame when it didn't turn out the way they expected. In your current or past relationships with a significant or romantic other, do you or did you get what you wanted?

> I learned to mother men and leave them when they did not become the father I wanted. I used, abused and abandoned men and/or I was used, abused and abandoned by men. I was sexually overactive.
>
> Louise

On your list of wants and expectations, how many of them are positive expectations? How many are negative? Is your list balanced or do you expect either all positive or all negative things to occur? No relationship is all positive or all negative. However, many adult daughters shared that their expectations, and in fact many of their relationships, were more negative than positive. What kinds of relationships do you have? Are they more positive than negative or vice versa?

No matter what your expectations, we know one thing is certain, which is that no relationship can make up for a lost childhood. No relationship can undo the past. You cannot put those expectations on your current relationships. If you do, you will burden your relationship with unrealistic expectations.

It is common for many adult children to talk about wanting to take care of their "inner child." This is that part of us which we often deny or were not able to experience joyfully when we were growing up. But remember it is *our* inner child. It is not the responsibility of your relationship person to treat your inner child. You are the best person to take care of the inner needs of your childhood and development.

If you do find someone who takes care of your inner child, you may find it initially comforting, but as you begin to grow, you will eventually find it confining and not how you want to be treated. Wanting someone to take care of the child part of you, will make it very difficult for you to be treated as an adult.

How realistic are your expectations? For example, some adult daughters talked about wanting to find the *perfect* man and thus had very high expectations. Obviously, very unrealistic ones too! However, if you are the perfect daughter, why not the perfect mate? These types of expectations will only lead to continual disappointment. You will find that neither you nor he ever lives up to your ideal.

Am I telling you to settle for less in your relationships? Absolutely not. Many adult daughters, however, shared that because their relationships never met their expectations, they perceived there must be something wrong with *them*. It is very possible that what was wrong was their distorted perceptions about what makes a good relationship and what they really wanted.

On the other hand, many adult daughters have settled
for less because they have become trapped in very controlling relationships. If your self-esteem is low, it affects
your opinion about the type of relationship you think you
deserve and will tolerate. You could find yourself expecting very little and tolerating a lot.

What Is A Healthy Relationship?

> I had a distorted perception of males. Mine was that men
> keep all feelings to themselves. I was lucky to marry a man
> "not just like my dad." But the first time he cried, I thought
> what a weak man. He's so dependent on me. Slowly I have
> come to realize that my husband is not my dad.
>
> Carmen

What is your definition of a healthy relationship? How
close are your actual relationships to your definition? Do
your expectations match your definition? Again we see
that great differences can occur. You may have a good
idea of what is a healthy relationship, but that does not
guarantee you will find one. More appropriately, knowing
what one is and being able to be healthy in a relationship
can be two different things.

If you were to write a list of characteristics to define a
healthy relationship, what would you include? Does your
list include any of the following?

- You feel you are respected as a person.
- Your physical and emotional needs are met.
- You like the other person and you feel liked by them.
- You are appreciated and not taken for granted.
- You are not afraid to be yourself.
- You can communicate effectively with your partner.
- You can affirm and support one another.
- Trust, trust, trust is everywhere.
- There is a sense of humor and play.
- Responsibilities are shared.
- Your privacy is respected.
- You are not constantly fighting for control.

- You or your partner admit and seek help for your problems.
- You want to spend time together.
- Love is a verb, not a noun.
- You are growing and the relationship is growing.
- You feel good about yourself.

Relationship Risk Factors

Are you susceptible to relationship problems? Adult daughters often felt that they were. What puts you at a high risk for troubled relationships? Adult daughters do not knowingly seek out relationship problems, but many find themselves in less than adequate relationships and are not sure how they got there.

The old belief that I'm only loved for what I do, not for who I am . . . the fear that I'll never be good enough.

Carrie

There are several factors that put adult daughters at a high risk for relationship difficulties. The most obvious one is your childhood in an alcoholic family. Additionally, gender socialization patterns contribute to one gender feeling more responsible for the success of a relationship than the other as we discussed earlier.

For example, your childhood and gender patterns might put you at risk because of your life experiences. You meet a person at your lowest emotional point and believe that ". . . he is going to take me away from all this." Not being taught by example because of your parents' relationship, you have little information about what makes a healthy relationship. Often this contributes to adult daughters being instantly and totally attracted to the first person who gives any emotional support. This person usually was not the best, but was the first for you.

People-Pleasing

If you were raised to think you had to be all things in a relationship to someone else, you were taught to expect very little, to tolerate inappropriate behaviors, to be "quiet" and you were taught to be a pleaser. These lessons put you at risk for getting into troubled relationships.

For example, what makes some adult daughters believe that they must be people-pleasers? Being a people-pleaser puts you at risk for getting into relationships that are out of balance, and you know who is carrying the load. If you are a people-pleaser, chances are you were raised to believe the following messages about yourself . . .

- Approval means love.
- You expect very little, but you are willing to give a lot.
- You care for others so that others will care for you.
- You become socialized to be dependent, eager to please and you fear abandonment.
- Everyone must like you.
- Being a perfect daughter makes you feel good about yourself.
- You care for others at the expense of not caring for yourself.
- You are invisible and caring at the same time.

If these beliefs and behaviors describe you, you are at risk for being a people-pleaser in your relationships. You are never pleased about your own needs. Most of the adult daughters who were in "pleasing-him" relationships were manipulated into believing that pleasing him would bring love and security. In reality, it brought him what he wanted, and them very little in return.

Karen Blaker tells us that people-pleasing doesn't work because it makes you vulnerable to a man, you never get true approval, it limits your capacity to accept love and it causes you to lose control (Blaker, 1988).

Choices

Another factor that puts you at a high risk for relationship problems is also related to your socialization patterns. ' When you think of a romantic relationship, what goes through your mind? Excitement, romance, challenge, physical attraction and mystery were often mentioned by adult daughters.

In their book *Smart Women, Foolish Choices*, Connell Cowan and Melvyn Kinder believe that many women are socialized to equate a relationship with excitement, challenges and meaning in their lives (1985). These are all wonderful feelings. If, however, these are the only ingredients in your relationships, it puts you at risk for ending up with less than healthy males.

Are you attracted to the kind of guys who are always slightly emotionally distant, who no one really understands but you, who definitely are mysterious, challenging (is an understatement) and who have an unpredictable side? Or are you attracted to guys who are very stable, predictable, nurturing and always loyal? In your head you know which type should be the best for you, but in your heart do you choose the emotional excitement? Are you usually attracted to these "mystery males," then wonder why your relationships are never satisfying? Now that is a mystery, isn't it?

Being Needy

Believing that you desperately need a relationship will also put you at a high risk for relationship problems. You will usually settle for less, be attracted to people who will use you and your fear of abandonment will put you at risk to be manipulated. When we are desperate for a relationship, our self-esteem is very low and we want guarantees in our lives. Ironically, it is at these times that we are most likely to get into relationships with the least healthy people. Eventually in these types of relationships your intense needs will betray you. They can become overwhelming to you and at the same time overwhelm the person in your relationship. Typically the response is for the other person to pull back. Your response is to try harder and harder. Desperately wanting a relationship, having intense needs, puts you at a disadvantage going into your relationship. It increases the probability of your being used and leaves you vulnerable.

Adult Daughters' Common
Relationship Problems

Besides being at a high risk for relationship problems, adult daughters shared their concerns about five specific problems they identified in their relationships. Not all adult daughters said they had all five problems. We will discuss each in the order of importance beginning with the most frequently mentioned.

1. Trust

When you are in a relationship how much should you trust? What should you trust the other person with? Do you trust yourself in relationships? Adult daughters stated that not only was the lack of trust the most common relationship problem, but also it occurred in many different forms.

For example, some adult daughters could not trust anyone else to meet any of their needs. These adult daughters believe they must maintain an emotional distance from others at all times in order to trust that they will not be vulnerable. At the same time they admitted their lack of self-trust made intimacy very difficult. Self-trust is related to "me phobia," which we discussed earlier.

Do you trust others with the real you? Do you hide the real you because you cannot trust you will be accepted or, more importantly, that you do not accept yourself and what you have to offer in a relationship? Lack of trust keeps us not only away from others, but also it keeps us locked in. Others cannot get emotionally in, and we cannot get out.

Other adult daughters shared that they didn't trust males or females at all. They stated that they were very distrustful when it came to their own or the opposite gender. Still other adult daughters did the exact opposite. For example, they were too trusting and gave their trust too easily. Have you ever found yourself more willing to trust new aquaintances more than people you already know? If you give your trust, do you give it totally and immediately? Obviously being either too trusting or not trusting enough puts you at a disadvantage in your relationships.

Finally, trust can be related to the problem of people-pleasing. Some adult daughters trusted that pleasing the other person will lead to their own happiness, but no, it just leads to trying to please the other person. Your happiness is not measured by their emotional state, it is measured by yours. Trust me. No, trust yourself.

Trust in a relationship begins with self, is shared with the other person, is received from the other person and is mutually experienced in the relationship. If you have trust problems in your relationship, it is because the sharing of trust is out of balance. This keeps you out of balance, more concerned with the other person and less likely to get your needs met.

2. Intimacy

The greatest intimacy problems shared by adult daughters had to do with either not allowing anyone to get close to them or not being able to become truly intimate with another person. Some adult daughters said they experienced both types of intimacy barriers in their relationships.

Do you keep people at a distance yet at the same time want someone you can be close to? Do you usually keep a certain emotional distance in order to maintain control, not to feel vulnerable, avoid the pain of rejection or because you fear intimacy? Many adult daughters admitted that having a truly intimate relationship was one of their major desires, but at the same time they expressed uncertainty about allowing someone to get "too" close to them.

Several feelings were behind their own internal mixed messages about intimacy.

For example, some adult daughters talked about their fear of being intimate. These adult daughters shared that their fears included fear of males, fear of the "price" of intimacy, not being able to bond with anyone, not being able to let go in their relationships, fear of rejection and a fear of giving yourself completely. Can you identify with any of these fears? If you are having difficulty with intimacy in your relationships, make a list of your fears in order to see what is holding you back.

> In my situation my fear of abandonment holds me back. It is something in my mind. I can see my behavior over the years has built these walls to keep him out. It's just something I am doing. So his saying, "I'm not going anywhere," is great but I have to solve the problem up here.
>
> Lea Ann

On the other hand we know that intimacy is a two-way street. Just because you are intimate does not automatically make your partner capable of healthy intimacy. However, as you might suspect, adult daughters who had intimacy problems in their relationships held themselves accountable for them and not their partners. Remember he can have problems that have nothing to do with you.

My friend, Kathy, told me that she and her boyfriend had a big argument about a month ago but that things were better now. Recently she said they were together and he was acting "differently." "What's wrong?" she asked, and he told her he was not feeling well. Being the good co-dependent, she was sure that he was not sick but that it was something that she had done. She kept questioning him about *her* behavior, refusing to accept that he was sick. Finally, he asked why she could not accept that he was just sick and that it had nothing to do with the relationship. You are not responsible for *his* problems! It is ironic that she didn't want to accept that he was sick. Just think of how many arguments you have had in your relationships and then mumbled to yourself, "He's sick!"

Therefore, other intimacy problems for adult daughters included having difficulty relating to their partners. Not being able to express their feelings was a barrier to achieving intimacy. What do you do with your feelings in your relationships? Do you keep them to yourself, share them with your partner or do you share them with someone outside of your relationship? In a healthy relationship you can share them with your partner. Most adult daughters stated that they did the other two.

For example, if you have a problem in your relationship, do you tell your best friend or confidant instead of your partner? Do you often fear that your partner would not understand or is not interested in your feelings? If so, you are in a relationship with intimacy problems. When this happens do you push the other person away before you can be disappointed by him or her? Do you keep your partner at a distance because you feel distant from him or her?

The last type of intimacy problems occurred as a mixed message for many adult daughters who expressed a strong desire to be left alone, but didn't want to be lonely. When did they most want to be left alone? Usually when their feelings were most intense and typically when they were negative feelings, such as feeling sad, upset, disappointed or hurt.

For example, when you have these feelings, is that the time you are most likely to withdraw in your relationship? It is ironic when you think about it, that this is the time you need the most support. If you cannot let another in, you cannot let your intimacy out. One of the most empty feelings in the world occurs when you need other people, want to need other people but do not know how to let them in.

Lack of achieving intimacy in your life can make you vulnerable to "love addiction" which can occur four ways (Cowan, 1985). You can become addicted to love out of longing, which is usually based on the lack of parental love. Wanting to be externally validated can lead to love addiction. You equate your self-worth with getting your partner's approval. Therefore, you must prove your "lovability" to him. When your relationship is based on the illusion that a male is your answer to intimacy, you are at risk for love addiction. He becomes a symbol to you of your value and thus you get trapped into the illusion of finding the perfect male. Finally, love addiction occurs when you are in love with being "in love." You become a romance addict.

3. Self-Worth

How can my husband love me unconditionally? How can I take the emotional hook out of my gut so I can learn to grow through the bad self-talk and bad history of personal worthlessness? I need to hear over and over and over to remap my life.

Janice

Closely related to achieving intimacy in your relationships is your opinion of your self-worth, which can affect your relationships in many ways. Adult daughters indicated that how and what they thought about themselves influenced not only how they acted in their relationships, but also influenced the types of relationships they were in. Do you feel that you are in a relationship that accurately reflects your self-worth?

If you have problems in your relationship, how good do you feel about yourself? If you don't feel very good about yourself, did this occur before or after your relationship problems? For example, when your self-worth is low, is that the time you are most likely to get into a dysfunctional relationship? On the other hand, if your relationship begins to have problems, does your self-worth drop?

It was not uncommon for many adult daughters to justify their relationship problems because they felt they did not deserve better. Having a low self-worth puts you at a great disadvantage for trying to find a healthy relationship. A low self-worth is not always obvious. You may believe you are very "together," but when relationship problems arise, you secretly feel you are not worthy of anything better and thus the problems are normal because of the type of person you are. As you can see, a low self-worth can lead to a relationship's self-fulfilling prophecy. This can occur when you expect what you feel you deserve and you get what you expect.

Other ways a low self-worth causes problems for adult daughters include never feeling good enough, not valuing yourself in your relationships, making poor choices about your partners, feeling inferior and feeling unlovable.

For example, do you feel different from other people and therefore expect to be treated differently? Does that mean that you expect to be given less than others in your relationships? Do you frequently find yourself observing other people's "healthy" relationships and with a deep breath wonder why you don't have one of those? (Where do those people come from who longingly gaze at each other on romantic cards in the gift shop?)

Another indicator of how self-worth influences your relationships is what happens to you when in the presence of your partner. Do you find yourself changing when "he" is around? We all adjust to the person in our relationship, but I mean do you become "small" when he is around? Do you feel that you lose whatever identity you have left? If so, this is happening because you don't feel good about yourself. This situation can be made much worse if you are in a relationship with a very dominant or controlling male. His dominance, coupled with your low self-worth, can keep you locked into a "little girl" relationship. He doesn't treat you as an equal and comes across more like your parent than your lover. You don't get the respect you should as a woman and are easily manipulated by him. One of the most destructive forms of manipulation that he can use is spouse abuse. Unfortunately too many adult daughters shared that they were caught in abusive relationships.

The lasting effects of low self-worth are why you continue to stay in a destructive relationship. Quite simply, low self-worth is like a magnet that holds you in. An adult daughter might stay in a dysfunctional relationship because of lack of energy to leave, fear of the future, waiting for the last straw, waiting for him to change. "It's not that bad," "For the sake of the children," "It's better than nothing," are all excuses that have been shared. However, whatever the reason, it can usually be traced to a low self-worth. One of the most common statements shared by recovering adult daughters was that as they became healthier, they demanded healthier relationships.

Raise your self-worth and you will raise your expectations in your relationships. More importantly, you will feel equal to your expectations. As your self-worth increases, your tolerance for inappropriate behaviors in your relationship will decrease. No partner can give you your self-worth, but if it is negative, he can use it against you to control you. A healthy self-worth contributes to develop and maintain a healthy relationship. It becomes the unspoken guideline for how the relationship will develop and grow. Self-worth is the ingredient for feeling good about yourself and your relationships. Without it, something very vital and healthy is missing in your relationships — YOU.

4. Responsibility

Who is responsible for the success of your relationships? Is it you, the other person or both of you? If you are a "good" adult daughter, you said it was you. If you want a good relationship, it should be both of you. I know, if you don't do it, it won't be right. If you don't do more than your share and assume most of the responsibilities, the relationship will fall apart, you say. Well, what does that tell you about the kind of relationships you get into or are currently in? It's bad enough to have too much responsibility in any relationship, let alone having to assume the responsibility for a dysfunctional one. However, feeling overly responsible for the success of a relationship was very strongly expressed by adult daughters in many ways.

For example, some adult daughters felt they just couldn't do enough in their relationships. This feeling was related to a fear that if they didn't do everything, things would go wrong. It was also related to control. Do you believe that if you assume most of the responsibility in your relationship and do enough, you can maintain control over the relationship? If so, you equate being responsible with being in control. This puts you in position for carrying the burdens of the relationship. Most of these burdens for adult daughters include trying to make everything okay for your partner all the time, being too loyal and living in fear of being abandoned.

I have difficulty relating to my husband. After 21 years of marriage, I still fear that if I make *one* mistake, all will be lost. Intellectually, I know that this is probably unlikely, but I fear this greatly.

Angela

Other adult daughters shared that their concerns about being overly responsible were very different. These adult daughters said they resented always having to be responsible. For example, do you ever get tired of everyone leaning on you or all the problems being dumped in your emotional lap? How do you feel about always having to be the strong one, the responsible one, or the I'll-take-care-of-it one? Are you the one who everyone comes to for advice, and you better be right? These types of responsibilities are very different from assuming that you have to do everything, these types of responsibilities are not only telling you that you have to do everything, but also expecting you to do everything.

The problem is my willingness to carry the burden of the relationship and realizing much later that much more giving than receiving occurred . . . and finally being angry that too little resulted.

Stacy

What about your expectations of responsibility in a relationship? Do you automatically expect that you will have to do more if the relationship is to be any good? Are you in a relationship with a person who is irresponsible, thus insures that you must be overly responsible? On the other hand, how good are you at sharing responsibilities in your relationships? For example, are you comfortable sharing responsibilities and sharing control in your relationships? Do you secretly believe that your partner cannot do things as well as you, therefore, you do it yourself?

If you are in a relationship where you are overly responsible, either by old habits or by not having a choice, you are in a relationship that is out of balance. Unfortunately you will be out of balance, too. When you overly identify with your partner by taking on the responsibilities of that person and your relationship, you underidentify with your responsibilities to yourself. In a healthy relationship you have a "personal bill of rights." In most relationships that are out of balance your rights are eroded gradually.

For example, in the beginning you may have given your willingness to do more than your share freely and lovingly but after a while, it becomes expected of you. Finally you feel used, taken for granted and you begin to not only resent all of the responsibility, but also your partner. Somewhere along the progression of your relationship, you lose your rights. You lose yourself. What a loss. Take your rights back. They're yours!

5. Picking The Wrong Person

To what kind of males are you attracted? Are you attracted to healthy males? Do you like being around them? Are you comfortable with them? Or are you attracted to males who you are not sure if they're healthy, but there is something about them that you can't resist? Do you get involved with males who initially you think are great, but then find yourself trying to either change or control them? Adult daughters stated that they were in relationships with all of the above types of males. Unfortunately, more were involved with males who did not treat them well and meet their needs than were involved with healthy males.

Mate-selection problems were ranked by adult daughters as the fifth most common relationship problem. I find it ironic that it was ranked fifth instead of first. However, if you look at the above four, they all pertain to characteristics of adult daughters. Thus even though adult daughters openly shared they have relationship problems, they still disproportionately hold themselves accountable for the problems. As we noted before, it is not uncommon for adult daughters to look at themselves first when something goes wrong. Although it is admirable to engage in self-examination, it can become unjustifiable self-condemnation. Obviously their partners had nothing to do with creating problems in their relationships! Don't excuse him for his share of the relationship problems. If you have relationship problems, don't just look in the mirror, look across the table.

Many adult daughters stated that they now recognize they did have a choice of relationship partners but many were not sure why they made such choices. Is it something about you or something about the males you choose, or both, that puts you at risk for picking the wrong person?

Many adult daughters shared that they eagerly looked forward to having a great relationship. They were aware of what an unhealthy relationship is from observing their parents. Armed with this knowledge, they believed that their relationships would be different, that they would be in loving and giving relationships, and that such relationships would be the answer to their childhood pain. Thus there was a strong belief among many adult daughters that "proper" mate selection would take them away from their emotional strife.

At the same time many adult daughters stated that they were very aware of what types of males they wanted to avoid. Obviously, those with alcoholic problems headed the list. Fear of getting involved with an abusive male was very high.

> I fear getting involved with someone who has a drinking problem. In fact, when I meet guys, one of my first questions is, "Do you like to go out?" . . . hoping their response is no because I correlate going out with drinking.
>
> Ingrid

Males who could not be there for them emotionally were to be avoided. We know that regardless of good intentions many adult daughters found themselves in relationships with types of males they wanted to avoid the most. Regardless of the type of male, whether alcoholic, abusive or emotionally distant, these males had one thing in common: They were very controlling.

If you have problems in your relationships, do you find yourself with very controlling males? Are you constantly fighting for control in your relationships? Do you try to become more controlling in order not to be controlled? Of all the problems that I have heard from adult daughters about their relationships, being in a relationship with a very controlling male was at the core of most of the problems. When you are controlled by him, regardless of his intentional or unintentional methods, you give up your identity, your needs, your self-worth and your chance at a healthy relationship. He controls not only your relationship, but also your emotions.

Are you in a controlling relationship? Check the following statements, written by Karen Blaker, to determine whether or not you are in a controlling relationship (1988).

1. When there's a problem in the relationship, he blames you.
2. He sometimes drinks too much and becomes physically or verbally abusive.
3. You know or suspect that he has been involved with other women.
4. He is late or stands you up for appointments or dates.
5. He forbids or criticizes your outside activities or hobbies.
6. He embarrasses you in front of other people.
7. He gets angry when you disagree with him.
8. He accuses you of flirting with other men when you are not.
9. He follows you to check up on you.
10. He is critical of the way you look or dress.
11. He insists on driving the car when you go out.

12. He has hit you.
13. He does or says things you never thought you would tolerate.
14. He stops talking to you or withdraws his affection when he wants to win an argument or make a point.
15. He says he needs his "freedom" or "space."
16. He has pushed you or twisted your arm or used some other physical act to make you bend to his will.
17. He doesn't allow you to have a checking account and gives you an allowance to pay the bills.
18. He uses sex to quiet your relationship doubts.
19. He is not interested in your day.
20. He gives you extra money or buys you presents when you have been "good."
21. He calls you a nag or accuses you of stirring up trouble if you want to talk about the problems in the relationship.
22. He never calls you by your real name — he uses a demeaning or derogatory nickname.
23. He doesn't phone when he is going to be late.
24. He wants you around when he is there.
25. He has been arrested at least once.
26. He feels uncomfortable or gets angry with you when you get attention (because of some aspect of your work or a special accomplishment).
27. He puts down your accomplishments.
28. He trivializes or makes fun of your feelings.
29. He often says you're too critical.
30. He flirts with other women in front of you.
31. He makes you feel sorry for him.
32. He frightens you with threats.
33. He finds fault with your friends and the people you are close to.

According to Karen Blaker if you answered yes to 20 or more of the statements, you are in a relationship with a very controlling male. If you answered yes to 12 or more, he is quite controlling. If you answered yes to five or more, he is somewhat controlling.

If you are in a controlling relationship, how did you get into it? Many adult daughters admitted they were attracted to certain males who eventually began to control them.

For example, some adult daughters were attracted to "needy" males and admitted they looked for males they could emotionally rescue. At the same time, they stated that in the beginning these relationships made them feel needed and useful. These types of males also need very high levels of approval. Initially, it made her feel important to him, but it soon became recognized for what it was, he needed to be the center of attention.

> I either look for men with weaknesses that I could rescue or I look for men who appear strong and would let me lean on them, only to discover they are dysfunctional.
>
> Camille

Other adult daughters said just the opposite. These adult daughters shared that they were attracted to males who appeared to be very strong and in control. For example, when they first met, the males came across as open with their feelings and would make statements that the adult daughters were thinking but were too afraid to express. Additionally, these males were usually dependable and self-assured. Finally, they were usually decisive and could take charge. These characteristics were initially attractive, but they were also the same characteristics that could be used to control others. Thus, the males were strong, but the adult daughters did not look far enough to see if they were also dysfunctional.

Once relationship problems emerged, many adult daughters stated they found it difficult to either work through the problems or to break free. The divorce rate for adult daughters as compared to women from non-alcoholic homes was 12% higher. Therefore, many adult daughters did get out, but it also tells us that many were not able to find resolutions to relationship problems.

Another problem arose for many adult daughters when they tried either totally to control their relationships, or if they were being controlled, tried to become counter-controlling. These adult daughters were in relationships with males who gave up total control to them. Again, at first this appeared to be attractive. However, it soon deteriorated into feeling they were taking care of a "little boy" and that they were asked to be more in the role of a mother than a lover or spouse. Resentment soon dominated these relationships.

Counter-controlling develops in your relationship as a response to being overly controlled and trying to fight back. Adult daughters who experienced these types of relationships shared that they were constantly fighting with or having to manipulate their partners not only to control his dysfunctional behaviors, but also to reduce his control over them. Unfortunately, either way these adult daughters were in a controlling relationship which was characterized by a constant power struggle.

Finally, there were adult daughters who were in very healthy relationships. Some of these adult daughters were well aware of the quality of their relationships and enjoyed them fully. Other adult daughters in healthy relationships admitted they had difficulty enjoying them. This was usually because of a fear that it would not last. Or a constant fear about whether or not they were doing the right things in the relationship. Their fear was that they would drive the other person away.

Whatever your current relationship, we know that being controlled, living with an alcoholic or living with some other type of dysfunctional person, is not what you deserve. You have a right to "relationship happiness." However, no matter how hard you try, you cannot be responsible for the happiness of your partner. You can support it, encourage it, share it but you cannot be it. You cannot do everything for the other person and make him happy. You can, however, lose yourself in the process and lose your own happiness.

Do adult daughters have healthy relationships? Yes. Can you have a healthy relationship? Yes. Think about this. One of the largest groups of people who are acutely aware of the power of healthy relationships and have a desire to be in them are adult daughters of alcoholics. Use your knowledge to lead you to what you want.

I opened this chapter by asking you what do you expect from your relationships and what is your definition of a healthy relationship? Raise your expectations. Find out what is healthy. Become the healthiest person you can be. Don't tolerate unhealthy behaviors and you will begin to establish the ingredients necessary for successful healthy relationships. Unhealthy and controlling males are trouble with a capital T. They will offer their controlling invitations to you and hope you will accept. Tell them you are too healthy to attend!

Avoid relationships that appear to have great potential if only he'll change. This means that you assume you can change him. He will continue to do what he does, but probably even more once you are in the relationship. Remember, he usually is on his "good" behavior when you first start dating. Stay clear of the "he'll-change" project. Remove the apostrophe from "he'll" change. I rest my case. The only one who will change is you and you will not like what you will become. As a matter of fact, you may become the exact opposite of what you wanted in your life. Becoming involved with a high risk male is the first step of the last thing you want to do. It is easier to meet someone who is right for you than to create him.

The power of a relationship can never be underestimated. The relationship you had with your parents while growing up is still with you. The hopes that a new relationship brings are tremendous. The love and beauty of a healthy relationship can add to your life beyond measure. But the devastation of a dysfunctional relationship may never end. Your quest for a healthy relationship, and being in a positive relationship, must always be in addition to your health and never a substitute for it. A healthy you is the first step to healthier relationships. Take care of yourself, have a positive relationship with yourself. You deserve it.

For me, I did not love myself, therefore, I could not genuinely love someone else. Today I love myself a little and, boy, am I reaching out! I can't wait until I love myself a lot. This may take one minute, one hour, one day or one year. That is not important, for I know it will come!

Rhonda

11

Perfect Parenting

What I have found myself doing is all the things I swore I would never do to my children and not knowing any other alternatives. This is especially true when I'm under a great deal of stress, which doesn't really have anything to do with my children.

Jessica

Next to relationships, problems about parenting were the second most important concern for adult daughters. Whether or not they had children, adult daughters expressed very strong opinions and emotions about their parenting skills. Their concerns ranged from not wanting children to wanting to be the perfect parent. Adult daughters who did not want children said they were afraid to have children due to emotional burnout from their own childhoods, lack of energy (or exhaustion) from having to parent themselves and/or their siblings while growing up.

Other adult daughters wanted children very much or already had children. Their concerns reflected their desires to want to be the best parents they could, wanting their children to have "normal" childhoods and a fear that they could not accomplish these things successfully. Whether they wanted children or not, the common bond among adult daughters about parenting was fear.

If you are a parent or think you will become one, what are your expectations and fears about parenting? Do you believe that you have the necessary skills to be a healthy parent? Do you want to raise your children totally different from how you were raised? Have you found yourself saying that you will never do to your children what was done to you? Are you afraid, however, that you might repeat the same family patterns of your childhood? If so, these are all very normal emotions for adult daughters.

This does not mean that adult daughters cannot be healthy parents. There are many healthy mothers who are adult daughters. It does mean, however, that adult daughters are acutely aware of not only their own childhoods, but also the influences from it that might be carried into their own parenting careers. These concerns led adult daughters to talk very openly about their feelings and anxieties about parenting.

Does this raise any concern you might have about your parenting skills? Nothing can put you in touch with your own childhood memories faster than being in charge of your children's childhoods. Maybe you don't remember much about elementary school, but when your child starts school, it will all come back.

For example, do you remember crayons and coloring in first grade? When you smell a crayon today, does it remind you of many years ago? More importantly, as you begin to parent and your child begins to respond emotionally, you will begin to feel again many of your own childhood memories. Your ability to work through your own childhood issues and separate them successfully from your parenting skills will be very important.

Your ability to parent successfully is related to your ability to give beyond yourself. We discussed this earlier when we talked about generativity. It is ironic that we have talked consistently throughout this book about adult daughters giving so much of themselves to others. It almost seemed at times as if adult daughters were saying that this is what they do best. When your talent of giving beyond yourself will be most needed, is that the time you express your greatest doubts about being able to do so successfully? All parents doubt their abilities. Adult daughters were very open about their doubts, but also shared some concerns that were definitely related to being an adult daughter not just a parent.

> I fear being like my mom. I fear destroying my child's self-esteem. I fear being too controlling, overprotective, then overcompensating and having no control. I fear my children hating me. I have no trust in my own judgment . . . . I expect perfection from myself and my kids.
>
> Cindy

Do you know what your parenting concerns are? Are you overly aware of trying to ensure that your children have a normal childhood? Do you try to do too much to make it normal thus unknowingly make it different for them anyway? Do you want your children to be able to express themselves and be free to try new behaviors, but at the same time expect them to be compliant?

Are you silently saying, "I want my children to have a different childhood than I did, but I expect them to behave the same as me?" This is not unusual for adult daughters. Research indicates that adult daughters who are parents have a higher expectation of compliant behavior in children than do women raised in non-alcoholic families who are parents. This is a mixed message for your children — be different, but be like me!

> I'm quick to use guilt and emotion, subtly used on me, to get desired results from my children.
>
> Lucille

Why do adult daughters expect so much obedience from their children? It is usually because as children themselves they were very compliant for fear of rocking the boat. They learned quickly to read other people and to be overly sensitive. Don't worry if your children are not like you. After all, this may tell you that you are doing a good job. In families not under stress, children don't have to be emotionally on guard and can do what they do best — be children.

Adult daughters expressed many concerns about their parenting abilities. We will discuss the most common four, beginning with the one that was mentioned the most. If you identify with these issues, you are probably a normal adult daughter who is expressing her normal parenting concerns. Now the challenge is to see if you can be a normal parent! (Don't worry, you don't have to be normal perfectly.)

1. Control

Not this again. It's everywhere. Control, control, control. Can't I get away from this? I don't know, can you? However, what I do know is that many adult daughters shared that their control issues interfered with their parenting skills. Do you have any control problems with your parenting? Do you know what they are?

> My own perfectionism and problems with the "child" part of me have caused my parenting problems. I find myself having difficulty having fun . . . . I find myself holding him back and not enjoying him as fully as I might. I have to consciously hold myself back and allow him freedom to *be*.
>
> Susie

Control problems affect parenting skills for adult daughters in several different ways. For example, many adult daughters admitted they wanted too much control over their children, but were afraid to let go. They exercised their controlling behaviors by taking on too many of the responsibilities for the children. Other adult daughter mothers expressed they found it difficult to allow their children to be free. They overly protected them, resulting in the adult daughter not being able to find a balance between "mothering" and "smothering" her children. Your overly developed need to control will impede their normal abilities to develop. Are you overly controlling? Ask yourself, do you allow your family to work out its problems or do you "take charge?"

> I struggle with needing to *overprotect* for fear of losing yet another precious part of me.
>
> Courtney

Control problems become evident when you believe you must be the "perfect parent." This is obviously a continuation of a role many adult daughters know well and have never abandoned. An indicator of this is taking your parental role too seriously. You learn to take care of your children quantitatively, but not qualitatively. Children need laughter, easy times, fun and many different ways of expressing emotions. Taking yourself too seriously not only takes these away from your children, but it also keeps them away from you.

Are you afraid you will damage your child if you make a mistake? Do you have a hard time telling your child "no" because you fear losing her love? Do you feel inadequate as a parent if you can't give everything? Are you afraid your child will not love you if you get angry with her or she gets angry with you? Do you find it difficult to accept that your children are less than perfect? Do you have incredibly high expectations for your children? Have your children, when upset, told you that they cannot be "perfect like you?" If so, you possess some of the indicators of needing a lot of control over your children. These are all indicators you are still having control problems as an adult daughter.

If you do have control problems, begin to work on them. Don't go overboard. Remember your children need many of your positive skills as an adult daughter in order to grow. They need your guidance, empathy, compassion and survival skills. They also need your love and support and they need their own emotional arena to use them. If you want your children's childhood to be different from your own, and you are having parenting problems, you may have to become different. The healthiest thing for a child is a healthy parent, not a controlling one.

2. I Don't Know How To Parent

Have you ever questioned your parenting skills because you were not sure of what you were doing? If so, not only are you like all parents, but this question is asked even more by adult daughters. Many adult daughters expressed that they just didn't trust their abilities to parent. This fear was usually related to the role-modeling they observed but which did not leave them with many skills about how to parent.

It was not uncommon to hear adult daughters share that they did not trust their parenting skills. This contributed to their fears that they would hurt their children by repeating many of the family patterns they most wanted to avoid. The ones they wanted to avoid the most were the behaviors that hurt them when they were young. However, many adult daughters felt that the only information they had about parenting was learned from their childhoods. This left them with a poor information system about how to fulfill their role as a healthy parent.

If you find yourself fearing that you do not know how to parent, what are your options? One, is do what you know, which is not what most daughters want to do. The other is to seek information about parenting. Involve yourself in parenting groups that teach healthy skills. Share your emotional concerns by joining parent support groups or in adult children of alcoholics groups.

There are many places to learn positive parenting techniques. Your local schools, colleges and community mental health centers often offer courses in parenting. Don't be afraid to go for help. Remember you want your children to trust you and they want to trust that you know what you are doing.

When we are uncertain about our parenting skills, we are often uncertain about normal behaviors in children. If you use your childhood as the encyclopedia of childhood behaviors, you will have a very limited knowledge of how "normal" children act. One of the most common problems for many adults who have problems parenting is that they usually have a very low level of knowledge about normal human development. Again, seek out resources in your community to increase your level of knowledge about children and what are normal behaviors.

I had to go to a parenting class and find healthy role models.

Claire

Gaining knowledge about normal human development will be a lot easier to accomplish when you get a realistic perception of what is normal. Additionally, learning what is normal parenting and normal child development will help you to overcome your perceptions that you must be the perfect parent and thus raise the perfect child. Hopefully you will find relief in discovering that all parents make mistakes, children don't always do what they should and yet healthy families still develop.

Besides perfectionism is not all that it is supposed to be. After all, when you're perfect, you have no place to go and very few people to whom you can turn. If you want your children to be healthy and want them to turn to you, let them know that you are human. Believing that you must be the perfect parent will always leave you doubting, make you lonely, make it very difficult for your children to get close to you, and no one, including you, will ever live up to your expectations.

3. Lack Of Consistency

How consistent are you as a parent? Is the "atmosphere" in your house consistent or does it shift unpredictably? Are you stable in your feelings towards your children or do you have "parental mood swings?" It was not surprising that many adult daughters talked about consistency problems in parenting. After all, how consistent was your house when you were growing up? Did things change instantly if one of your parents came home drinking? Did the mood of your family shift to reflect the unpredictable moods of your parents?

Parental inconsistency for adult daughters can be divided into two categories. These are mood (or feeling) inconsistencies and behavior inconsistencies.

For example, some adult daughters shared that they could not control their mood swings and that it caused them to be either too loving sometimes and too distant at other times. Other adult daughters indicated that they had a hard time staying in their parenting role.

> My daughter has parented me most of her 17 years.
>
> Sheila

Some adult daughters stated that they could be there physically for their children, but were not always emotionally present. Many adult daughters questioned their abilities to be fair with their children. Although all parents would like more patience, adult daughter parents openly expressed that they often vacillated in how much patience they had. This led many to question whether or not they were consistent with their feelings with their children.

On the other hand, it was not unusual to find that many adult daughter parents expected their children to be consistent in *their* behaviors and moods. Many stated they found it very difficult to allow their children to express different moods, always wanting their children to be content. When the children even voiced normal anger or anxiety, it often created disproportionate anxiety in the adult daughter because of her desire to want to control everything. Someone else's anxiety can make you very uncomfortable if you think it's your fault or that you should do something about it.

Finally, inconsistency fears were related to adult daughters' difficulty in accepting differences between their children and themselves in behaviors, feelings and attitudes. When you expect your children to be like you, and they are not, it is inconsistent with your expectations. Some adult daughters were afraid that if they showed their disapproval for different behaviors, they would inhibit normal autonomy in their children. Others talked about how inconsistency interfered with their bonding with their children.

4. Not Being Able To Meet Your Child's Needs

> My lost childhood and I do not have the energy or a heart big enough to really be the parent I feel a child should have.
>
> Ellen

Do you ever fear you cannot adequately nurture your child? Are you afraid you cannot meet your child's emotional needs? Do you ever wonder if you are ignoring your child's needs? Do you feel you cannot provide for your child's needs because yours were not met? If so, you share some very common concerns with other adult daughter parents.

Not being able to meet a child's needs was expressed in several different ways by adult daughters. Some were concerned they could not love unconditionally. Others were not sure they could express openly their approval to their children.

Some adult daughters believed they could meet their child's needs if they just protected the child from unpleasant things. Wanting the child to meet your needs was not uncommon for some adult daughters. The desire to have someone love us, need us and rely on us is strong. On the other hand, we must remember to reciprocate. Related to this problem is when you see your children as a second chance for your childhood. Unfortunately trying to re-live yours through theirs will not help your children. However, you can have a healthy parenthood by enjoying your child.

Sometimes the key to healthy parenting is to make sure we grow up before our children do. You will find that as you meet your children's needs, your needs as a parent will start to be met. This does not mean that everything will be smooth. It does mean, however, you can achieve a balance of needs in your relationship with your children; but not a fifty-fifty relationship exchange. Your children need a lot from you. A balanced exchange is when you can give as much as you can and still maintain your emotional health. At the same time your children make you feel every now and then glad to be a parent. Notice I said every now and then. We have three children, but on some days I feel like they have us. Obviously, some days as parents we are tired and exhausted, but that does not mean we are tired of our children. We try to do the best we can.

Remember, you are allowed to meet your needs as well. We become out of balance as parents when we forget that. When you are trying to get your needs meet, remember you have adult needs and children cannot meet all adult needs. Your needs as an adult must be met by other adults and you.

Did you identify with the above concerns of adult daughter parents? I am sure you can add to the list of problems, fears and emotions.

Something I would like to add, which puts additional pressure on adult daughters, is the current social pressure to become "superwoman." The media image that you must do absolutely everything for your children, your relationships, your profession, your body, your mind and do it all with a smile on your face, will leave you totally burned out.

I recently saw an article that said in order to have a "good day" you need 42 hours! (*USA Today*, 1989.) According to this article we're even supposed to set aside time each day for "meaningful interaction" with our plants! Information and pressure like this will make you not only exhausted, but also disappointed in yourself because you cannot be and do all things. Superwomen aren't supposed to have good days, they are supposed to have "perfect days." This only leaves you feeling as if you don't have enough time in your day. It leaves you feeling that you can never do enough. If you allow yourself to succumb to the pressure of "superwomen," you will feel that your only solution is to try even harder. You will become burned out on parenting very quickly. Parenting is for life. It is not a life sentence. (Although some days . . .) Conserve your energy and use it wisely. Do not become consumed by the superwoman image. When your parenting energy is consumed, it must be replaced. You cannot replace it by becoming a better parent, but you can replace it by taking better care of yourself, which will help make you a better parent.

As adult children we are extremely aware of the influence that family has on children. We are extremely aware of how important healthy relationships between parents and between parents and their children are. However, we must be aware that we are at risk for extreme self-criticism and self-doubt about our parenting skills. It is okay for us to say that we want to do a good job, but at the same time we are not sure of what we want to do. We tell our children to try alternatives, express their feelings, act their ages and have fun. If this is such good advice, maybe we should try it ourselves. Don't let your unresolved childhood issues or fear of parenting skills hold you back.

You are probably a much better parent than you think. You may have behaviors that put you at risk, but you also have some of the greatest assets to be a healthy parent. You have a desire to want to do a good job. You have the ability to recognize needs in others. You are not afraid to become involved. You know the power of parents.

Do you want to be a healthy parent? If so, work through your doubts, find resolution to your own childhood issues, learn appropriate parenting skills and use those parts of you that are healthy. All children need guidance, love, support, nurturing and acceptance. So do parents.

> The most important thing about my relationship with my daughter is that I allow her to be herself and I appreciate her for what she is. As I watch her grow, the most valuable part of my parenting is having her appreciate who she is, having her love herself . . . having her feel she has a right to be

here and to ask for what she needs to be happy. It's okay to
be just the way she is . . . . It's okay to be angry and it's okay
to do the wrong things and that Mama's going to love you
anyway. No matter what you do. And she does have that
attitude about herself.

Evelyn

PART FOUR

Discovery And Recovery
Of Me

12

I Think I Can, I Think I Can

Remember the story of "The Little Engine That Could?" The little engine was asked to pull all of the train cars over the mountain because the big engine broke down.

"I can't do it because I'm too small," wailed the little engine and did not want to help. The other cars, however, told the little engine that if it did not help, they would not be able to get over the mountain. At this point it becomes a co-dependent story. All of a sudden the responsibility for the big cars is placed on the little engine. So what does the little engine do? It allows itself to get talked into trying and co-dependently begins to pull the other cars up the mountain. The entire time it is pulling it is telling itself "I think I can, I think I can." It is not sure it can do it but since it is for someone else, it is willing to expend all of its energy trying. Eventually the little engine makes it to the other side of the mountain and discovers that it has great strength.

Are there any similarities between this story and you?
Can you make it to the other side of the recovery mountain? Do you realize that even though you have been
pulling the weight of others for so long, you have great
strength? Do you realize that even though you may have
been doing things co-dependently, you are capable of making transitions in your life to meet your own needs? Have
you discovered your strengths, capabilities and spirit
which you can now use for yourself? Have you ever
thought "I think I can, I think I can" about your own
potential for recovery?

Throughout this book we have been on a journey of
discovery and recovery. What have you discovered about
yourself? Do you have a better understanding of who you
are and what you would like in your life? Do you want to
change? Will you change? Will you buy a ticket on the
recovery train or will you sell them to others? As an adult
daughter you have something today that you did not have
in childhood. You have a choice. You can stay where you
are. You can keep those things you learned painfully that
serve you well today. You can work through and learn to
let go of your grief and losses. You can build upon your
strength. You do have choices. Will you use them?

I will not tell you what to choose or what to change.
You are the explorer who is discovering herself. On your
journey you are identifying those places you do not want
to visit again. You are also finding those places in you
that are warm, confident and full of hope you will want
to visit over and over again to find more energy to
further your journey. Will I tell you how to travel? No,
but I will share the map that many recovering adult
daughters shared with me.

Desire For Change

Do you have a desire to change your life, your attitudes,
your feelings? Would you like to be free of the emotional
baggage that you carry as an adult daughter? Do you find
yourself wondering why you cannot enjoy life as much as

you would like, but admit you would like to try? If so, you are not alone. Besides all the issues we have discussed so far, the desire for change was equally strong among adult daughters. As perceptive, intuitive and empathic as adult daughters were about others, I found them to be equally energetic about their own behaviors and feelings once discovered. However, they were more likely to use their emotional skills on others than on themselves.

Can you convert your desire for change into action? Many adult daughters did and were willing to share their insights. Recovering adult daughters shared five common nuggets of advice they would offer other adult daughters. These were:

Use your past.
Take care of yourself.
Find out what you have missed.
Get into a recovery group.
Find healthy people to be around.

Use Your Past

Do you realize your past can be a tool for recovery? You can convert your survival skills into growing skills. Don't be afraid of your past but don't allow it to become "eternal." Because once you were affected negatively, are you saying you will always be affected negatively? The only thing that can make our past worse is allowing it to continue to affect us negatively.

For example, I am an adult child and I will be one until the day I die, but I will not die one more day because I am an adult child. What about you? Are you through giving up your days to the past?

Your traumatic childhood is over. Yes, the pain can still be there but you can use your strength to break its hold on you. You were victimized by alcohol, don't be victimized by your past. We must remember to keep the label of ACoA in perspective. It tells us where we have been. It should not predict where we are going. If the label predicts, we are co-dependent on the label.

Read, learn and grow but don't use the ACoA label as an excuse for being dysfunctional. Don't become immersed in ACoA issues to the point where it becomes a dysfunction itself.

Stella

Take Care Of Yourself

How many times have you told yourself, "I better take care of _____ "? Up until now it has always been someone else's name. Recovering adult daughters are telling you to put yourself first. They are telling you to take care of yourself. You do not have to be a caretaker. You are not in charge of the universe. You are only in charge of yourself. What do you do for yourself? Can you make a list of how you take care of yourself? Could you convince someone who is concerned about you that you are taking good care of yourself?

You can care without being a caretaker for everyone. You have to put yourself first and not last. To be self-caring is not selfish.

Glenda

Be kinder to yourself. Learn to let go of the unrealistic expectations that you place on yourself. You have a right to your own needs and exercising your rights is the first step towards taking care of yourself.

The best statement that I know for adult daughters is written in the _Desiderata_ and it simply and eloquently states, _"You have a right to be here."_

Taking care of yourself means you are taking responsibility for your own growth. Do not fear your growth. Do not put it off because you fear it will be painful to work through your feelings. Remember, growing pains are less severe and more healthy than past pains. Give yourself time to change. True change is measured in small steps; measured in what you do daily.

As you begin to take care of yourself watch out for depression. It is normal to feel the emotions of working through your past. It is normal to find yourself getting angry over things you have denied for a long time. When you start to feel overwhelmed by what you have discovered about yourself or by your journey of recovery, slow down. No one said you had to recover perfectly. No one said you must forgive every transgression in your life. It's your journey. You're the engineer and if you start to feel depressed, find a rest stop.

Taking care of yourself means putting your needs first. This is a very unusual behavior for many adult daughters. Take your time. It will be easier to take care of yourself when you feel better about yourself so take the time to do things that will make you feel good about yourself.

Recognize What You Have Missed

Discovery is not only recognizing how you were victimized, but also realizing what you have missed. Are you aware of what you have missed? More importantly, are you willing to try to get it now? The greatest pain from the past continues when it keeps us from getting what we missed.

My hope for the future is just to have peace. One of the big secrets of my program is not to look ahead . . . to try, except for necessary planning, not to even look to the next hour, but to savor the moment. That's not something I've ever done in my entire life. I lived my whole life planning and building walls and trying to avoid disasters that were inevitable. Now I've learned to just savor the moment. To accept whatever life is offering me now. It's not that I don't have hope, it's just that I have faith that when tomorrow comes, whatever it is, it's going to be right for me. That allows me to enjoy today.

Harriet

When you become aware of what you want because it is missing in your life, you begin to find a purpose and a direction for your recovery. Getting what you have missed can be a goal. Becoming the kind of person you would like to be gives you direction. If you are not sure of what you want to do, don't spend all of your energy trying to figure it out before you begin your recovery.

You can start right now by asking yourself, what *don't* you want to do? Many times knowing what we don't want can lead us in the right direction.

For example, if you don't want to stay as you are, you don't want to be isolated, you don't want to keep the family secret to yourself, you don't want to keep having relationship problems and you don't want to keep all the pain inside anymore, you have found out a lot about yourself. You can use this self-discovery to begin your journey, just as much as you can use your knowledge of how you would like to change. The important thing is to start your journey, not decide on your destination. Don't add "missing the journey" to your list of what is missing in your life. All you have to know is that when you ask, "Do you know what is missing in my life?" you answer, "Recovery and I'm going to find it."

Growing In Groups

We did the best we could, but we did it alone — no more.

Ginny

You don't have to recover alone. As a matter of fact, you will recover faster and better with the help of other people. One of the best ways to overcome feelings of uniqueness and isolation is to be with other people. Find a good support group and get involved. There are many options available to you. You can go to Al-Anon meetings for adult children. You can find independent ACoA groups. You can try women's support groups. You can get involved in counseling or therapy groups. The important thing is that you get involved in a group.

You will be better able to confront your feelings when you are surrounded by people who understand not only you, but also the dynamics of alcoholic families. Don't be afraid to ask a counselor what she or he knows about adult children issues. If she is not comfortable with or knowledgeable about adult children, find someone who is. Remember you are the consumer of your recovery — ask for what you need.

What I'm hoping to accomplish from being in this group is to find out who I am and what I like to do. I know some things, but a lot of the things that I think and believe seem to be things I picked up from my dad . . . . I don't really know if that's me. So I am trying to understand me and I am still discovering.

Nan

If you try a group and your needs are not being met, don't give up on the idea of growth through groups. Try another group. In fact, I recommend that you try at least six different groups before you think about giving up. We are still learning how to meet the needs of adult children and mistakes are being made. Some adult groups are not as healthy as others. After all, no one said that adult support groups have to be perfect. As a matter of fact, maybe it is the one who is trying to be perfect that is the least healthy. If your group reminds you of your alcoholic family, find another group.

Remember, not everything you are looking for in recovery, will be in an adult children's group. You can be emotionally supported by your adult children's group, but you can attend other groups to learn further skills.

For example, you can learn relationship and communication skills, self-esteem techniques, assertiveness training and parenting skills in a variety of other types of support groups and training workshops.

Remember, you don't have to alcoholize all of your recovery. You are much more than an adult daughter and you have a diversity of talents and needs. Growth is for all parts of you. But in many cases it has been the "adult daughter part" that has held you back. Go and do it all. Become the healthiest you, not the healthiest adult daughter!

Find Healthy People

As you discover yourself, you will find you no longer will tolerate unhealthy behaviors. The healthier you become, the more aware you become of unhealthy people.

One of the best ways to learn healthy behavior is to be around healthy people. This will become very important to you as you begin to change.

For example, those people who know you the best as an adult daughter, are often the ones who will be the most resistant to the new you. They share a common history with you, they have relied on you to meet their needs, they need you to be in your supporting role. Now you are taking the lead role and they are not sure of how to react. What will they do? Usually they will do what they do best, which is to respond to you in their old ways. Will you fall back into your old habits or will the recovering you step forward?

For example, one of the best indicators of discovery and recovery is wanting to share what you have found. Where do most adult daughters want to share their growth? Usually in their relationships or with their families of origin. You visit your family and they are playing the same old dysfunctional song. What do you do? Do you sing along? After all, you know the words by heart. Or do you learn to respond differently? They will always try to pull you back because that is the person they know best, the old you. Besides the old you meets their needs. They will try to push your buttons. This is not unusual because they installed them. It will be easier for you to know when to separate yourself from unhealthy behaviors when you have healthy friends and relationships to go to.

It is not your responsibility to make your family healthy. Don't get trapped into the role of family counselor. Be on guard for this. Once you start to grow and deal with the alcoholism in your life, you become the new family expert. They will try to use you by pulling you back, trying to manipulate you with all the old emotional buttons.

Discovery and recovery take time. You will pass through different stages on your journey of growth. Each stage will have benefits but will also have traps that can keep you from going further.

For example, don't confuse recovery with something else. Don't confuse it with discovering things about yourself. Don't confuse recovery with awareness. When you first discover that many of your behaviors are normal for an adult daughter, there is a sense of relief. You feel better about yourself. This is a discovery step, not a recovery step. Don't confuse relief for recovery. When you are injured and the pain stops, we feel relief, but that does not mean that we are better.

Each stage of discovery brings relief. Enjoy it. Use it to gather energy for the next stage and then go on. You deserve recovery. Don't settle for anything less. This is one time you have the right to ask for everything. As you go through the different stages be cautious of the "awareness trap." This can occur when you become so preoccupied with wanting to recover perfectly, and learn all of the proper steps, that you lose sight of your reasons for recovery. You become so trapped into memorizing and learning the *process* that you forget the *end* results. The idea of recovery is to get there, not memorize the way.

Stages Of Recovery

As you attempt to change you will probably go through several stages which include:

Recognition

The first stage of recovery is the recognition of the movement of recovery from alcoholism. This movement has expanded so much in the last several years that it is touching millions of people for the first time. It is not only a movement of recovery, it is a movement of community. You will recognize the community and more importantly you will realize that you want to recover and become part of this community.

You will recognize that how you were influenced and how you are living is not what you want. You will recognize that alternatives are available and that you want to try them. You will recognize the most important part of recovery — yourself.

Involvement

Involvement in recovery can occur two ways. These are intellectually and emotionally. Most adult daughters shared that they had no problems becoming involved intellectually with recovery.

For example, they wanted to learn everything there was to know about adult children, alcoholism, dysfunctional families and troubled relationships. They were willing to read all of the books (thank you for buying *this* book), attend all of the ACoA conferences they could find and discuss the "issues" for hours. As adult children, if we could recover by doing it intellectually, we would have the healthiest minds in the world!

Most adult daughters were not afraid to say what they "think." Many had problems, however, not only identifying their emotions, but also expressing them.

Involvement in your recovery requires that you become emotionally involved. You cannot recover by what you know. You recover by feeling what you know. If you are afraid of your feelings, you will be afraid of being involved. Adult daughters were very open about the emotional barrier to recovery that many of them were behind. It is much easier for us to rationalize, minimize and intellectually justify our pain than it is to feel it and work through it. Don't confuse knowledge with emotions. Otherwise you will "know" recovery, but never "feel" it.

Wanting To Change

As you become more aware of yourself and your alternatives, you become more aware of wanting to change. However, make sure you are aware of the direction in which you would like to change. Don't get caught in the cycle of wanting to change everything about yourself. After all, you have many admirable qualities that got you this far. Don't throw the best parts of you away because you think that you must change everything.

Additionally, change takes time. You have been an adult daughter for many years so give yourself time to change. You don't have to do it all at once, nor do you have to do it completely. You set the pace. If you put too many expectations on yourself in too short a time, you will do the exact same thing that everyone else did to you for so long.

> Have patience . . . you must give time. We didn't get sick overnight and we're not going to get better overnight. Nurture your strengths. You are a survivor . . . be very patient and gentle with yourself . . . go slow, determine what works for you. Take it easy and don't rush.
>
> Tessa

Finding Help

When you first find help, you will validate your awareness. You will find a lot of comfort when you realize that many of your feelings and ideas are shared by others. However, this is where many adult daughters reached the "discovery plateau" and didn't know how to go any further. They entered into support groups, discussed their lives, feelings, doubts, needs and emotions, but were not able to change their insights or the support they received into action. This was not uncommon. I found that many adult children who went into support groups stayed at the same level of awareness about their problems and were unable to find a way to change their lives (Ackerman, 1989).

When you find help, make sure you also find a way to convert the support you are receiving into ways for you to recover. Knowledge, without a way to use it, creates frustration. You have lived enough frustration in your life by not being able to change others. You can, however, avoid developing frustrations about yourself by turning your knowledge into actions.

Living Your Recovery

> To feel the spirituality in me is the peace and joy that I wake up with in the morning and that I carry with me throughout the day. The joy in my heart to be alive . . . that's a real blessing for me. I'm grateful to be alive and I

never was before. That's my sense of spirituality . . . To
know God is with me and forgives me, even before I am able
to forgive myself.

Anne

Recovery is for living not discussing. The last stage of
recovery is applying what you have learned. Again, you
do not have to do this all at once. One of the most obvious
things to many adult daughters was that the very characteristics of adult daughters are the worst ones to have
when it comes to recovery. Perfectionism, denial, control,
over-responsibility, lack of trust and a low self-esteem are
not the qualities that recovery is built on. As a matter of
fact, they can be your worst enemies.

An important part of recovery is called "recovery lag"
(Ackerman, 1987). This means that not all parts of the
adult daughter are affected negatively, not all parts will
need the same amount of intervention and not all parts
will recover at the same rate. Some parts of your recovery
will take longer than others. It's normal. After all, some of
your issues are more emotional and more painful than
others. They will need more time. Recovery is not a
contest. You don't have to do it perfectly and you don't
have to do it better than everyone else.

Finally, recovery is for yourself. Many adult daughters
felt it would be easier to recover for someone else than for
themselves. Maybe it would. The problem is we will never
know. You cannot recover for another person and no one
can recover for you. Not that we haven't tried. There are
a lot of co-dependent traps along the way to recovery.
Keep the focus on yourself and you will avoid them.

What is the goal of recovery? You are. The object of
recovery is not only to *find* yourself, but also to *be* yourself. Use whatever you can to find recovery. Use the
strengths that you have developed, even if they were co-
dependent, to pull yourself up your own mountain. Find
the other side of your mountain. Find the other side of
you. Don't stop yourself because you feel small. Don't

become overwhelmed by the journey and don't worry where it will lead. The important thing is to begin.

When is the best time to start your journey? Now. What are you waiting for, someone else's permission? Tell them to keep their co-dependency to themselves. You have a very important place to go. You've got your ticket, you've got your emotional baggage, you've got your strength and you've got your map. Now go. Find your recovery land!

I think I can, I think I can. I knew I could, I knew I could.

If I am not for myself, who will be for me?
If I am not for others, who am I for?
And if not now, when?

from The Talmud

13

To Self, With Love, From Daughter

Can you make the transition from being an adult daughter of an alcoholic to being your own person? Can you make the transition from co-dependence to independence? Can you leave the shadow of the past to find your place in the sun? Is your identity dependent upon where you have been, or is it developing and changing to meet where you are going?

Yes, yes, yes, you can do all of these things. You can become your own person, overcome co-dependent behaviors and find balance in your life. However, how will you know when you have become your own person? How will you know you are no longer dominated by your past and you are becoming a healthy adult?

Your answers will depend not only upon your perceptions of recovery, but also upon your ability to live your recovery. For example, if someone accused you of recovering, could they find enough evidence to convict you? We know that you intellectually understand the issues of adult daughters. We know you can change if you want. We know you have choices. We don't know, however, if you will change enough to become your own person.

Becoming your own person will require using all of your adult daughter skills to care for a very special person. It will require you to transfer your caregiving, nurturing, responsible behaviors and spirit to the one person who can use them the most. You will give them to the one person who will cherish forever your gifts that you painfully learned as an adult daughter. You and your gifts will be used to create not only a person, but also a healthy sense of self within this person. The gifts will demand a heavy price from you, for once they are given, they will take away your identity as an adult daughter. Thus your gifts are the ultimate you can give.

Is there such a person who is worthy of these gifts from you? Is there anyone in the world who deserves your giving up your current identity? There is only one person. She is an adult daughter herself. She is you. Allow your adult daughter to give up herself in order to create a magnificent sense of self. It is a gift from her to you. It is a gift of self. It is the gift of recovery.

You now become the creator of who you choose to be. You now can pick up your emotional brush and paint your portrait. Your adult daughter brings all of the colors and all the paint. You bring the canvas and the idea of your image and together you can create the healthiest self possible. You can create your life now. Do you know what you want to become? Will you pick up your brush? Will you find your self?

What Does Recovery Mean To You?

You know the kind of person you are now. If you would like to change, what would the new you look like? How would you like to feel? Would you keep some of your old emotional parts? How many new emotions would you have? Make a list of what you would like to be like in your recovery. Include how you would like to live, to express your emotions and how you can learn to receive intimacy from others. Once you have this picture, you have some idea of what you mean by recovery. Now the problem is how to get there.

You will find that you can achieve your recovery if you include some of the following ingredients:

Recovery Includes Letting Go

You cannot hold onto the past and expect to grow in the future. You cannot keep your identity as an adult daughter as your only identity. The recovering person is not past oriented, but growth oriented. As you recover you will begin to let go of pain, emotions and barriers that have held you back. Keeping all of these inside of you will usurp your energy. As you let go, you will find new energy for your recovery. What a relief and a joy it is when we are able to let go of our negative emotional baggage. The only thing that can hold you back and keep you from letting go is yourself. It is your recovery and you are free to let go of those things you no longer want as part of your new self.

Recovery Includes Balance

Do you remember back in Chapter Six when you identified many of your adult children characteristics? Recovery does not mean that you must completely change or become the exact opposite of your characteristics. It means that you can find balance in your life. Many of your characteristics can be changed to assets in recovery.

A recovering person has balance in her life. You are able to meet your needs, feel good about yourself, care and identify with others as a healthy person and not feel used by others. Your previous life was out of balance. Your new self is searching for balance. Your old adult daughter was willing to go to any limits to accommodate a lot of unhealthy behaviors which kept you out of balance and a stranger to yourself. The new self knows who she is and how to maintain her balance. We don't completely throw away where we have been. To do so would make us out of balance. We are where we have been. Keep your strengths to keep your balance but balance your strengths with your recovery to find yourself.

Recovery Includes Healing

Do not be afraid to face your pain or admit your injuries. You must heal yourself as you recover. There is no such thing as recovery that includes maintaining old wounds. Your healing will require you to admit injuries and to forgive those who have injured you.

I do not presume to tell you that you must forgive all the injuries in your life. I have heard too often from victims that some things are not forgivable. It is not my place to judge your need to forgive. However, if you choose to forgive, make your forgiveness a part of your healing. Don't forgive because someone else told you to. If you do, your act of exoneration will be co-dependent. Relate your forgiveness to your recovery. Ask yourself, "How will forgiving help me to heal?" When you find your answer, you will know what to do with forgiveness.

Healing takes time, so does recovery. Do not be too anxious. When you are injured and you return to your normal activities too soon, you risk being injured again. Be patient with your recovery. They are your wounds so give them the best care possible. The healing recovering person knows when she can move on. She will know because she is beginning to take care of herself. You cannot find recovery without going through the healing process. If you rush through it, not heal through it, your old emotional wounds will call you back. Recovery without healing is a placebo. Healing and recovery is a good prescription. Remember the medicine to find your cure.

Recovery Includes Giving

Recovery means you are able to find all of the things you have missed, then give them to yourself. Recovery is a gift of self. It is no wonder so many recovering people feel as if they have been emotionally reborn. They have found the gift to enjoy their lives fully. Who has your gift? It is not on this page. It is in your hands. It is in your heart, your spirit, your emotions, your recovery.

Can you find your gift, and if you do, can you open it? Do you know what is inside? I do. It is all the things you lost or had taken from you when you were a little girl. They are all the things you put into your secret emotional hiding place. Many adult daughters have been secretly carrying the gift every day, hoping that they could open it, only to find that one more day went by and the gift remained wrapped. Other adult daughters, like the princess in the story, have forgotten where they put their emotions and childhood spirit. Your gift has been under lock for a long time. Have you found your keys? More importantly, have you found the locks to let yourself out?

The keys to your recovery are inside you. Open your locks and receive your gift. When you can give to yourself, you will find no one can ever take it away again. You will no longer hide who you are. You will find that recovery is not only giving, but also the repetition of receiving. You will never grow tired of opening your gift of recovery because it will always contain new presents for each new day. To recognize and appreciate your presents, you must be recovering enough to not only know what they are, but also to enjoy them. When this happens, you will know you have given yourself the gift of recovery.

Developing Your "Self"

How do you know that not only are you recovering, but also that you are making the transition from adult daughter identity only to developing a healthy sense of self? You will know it when you begin to believe and feel that you can be yourself without fear. You will know it when you can celebrate yourself, when you begin to like yourself and when you can make peace with yourself. You will know you are getting better and developing a healthy sense of self when you start to do some of the following:

- You no longer feel you have to be controlling.
- You begin to have the kinds of relationships you always wanted.
- You begin to feel more and think less about your emotions.
- You no longer fear your memories.
- You have internally made peace with those who have harmed you.
- You trust your own judgments.
- You no longer live in fear of "me phobia."
- You are able to affirm your qualities.
- You no longer think of yourself as an adult daughter only.
- You are beginning to respect yourself.
- You are learning to like and love yourself.
- You can receive love and intimacy from others.
- You can say no to others and yes to yourself.
- You learn to embrace the spirit of recovery.

All of these are indicators of making the transition from adult daughter to becoming your own person. The more you recover the closer you will be to developing a healthy self. Recovery and developing a healthy self have one thing in common, which is they are both continual processes. Neither of them is a destination. They are both magnificent journeys. How disappointing it would be to limit your recovery and your personal growth. As an adult daughter you have been very restricted in your identity and behaviors but no one can now restrict your growth but you.

Learning To Like Yourself

The most devastating impact from alcoholic families is that they produce people who do not like themselves. Your greatest transition challenge will be to learn to like and to love yourself. If you do not like yourself, you will find it harder to live with yourself than with an alcoholic. You have proven you can tolerate dysfunctional behavior from someone else, but you will not tolerate it from yourself. When you begin to like who you are, you will open an entire emotional world that has been closed to you. Learn to like yourself. After all you are going to spend a lot of time together!

When you like yourself, you will be able to celebrate yourself as a survivor, not a victim. You will be able to enjoy humor, not painful sarcasm. You will trust your decisions because you will like who makes them. When you like yourself, you respect yourself. You will improve your relationships because you will feel you deserve the best and have a lot to offer. When you like yourself, you will make the transition from being a *perfect daughter* to becoming the *perfect you*. You will realize and accept that the perfect you includes all of you, the positive and the negative, and that's okay. The perfect you is not co-dependent. The perfect you is not controlled by others. The perfect you is not afraid of herself. You are the best at being you. No more imitating someone else. No more seeing yourself through their identity. When you like yourself, you can *be* yourself.

Learning To Receive

Your greatest barrier to recovery and self-growth will be your inability to receive. Break down that barrier. Let your feelings out and recovery in. Don't allow yourself to journey so far then deny yourself entrance into your healthy land. You have given so much, but still you feel empty. You must be able to receive what you want in order to change. If you want to feel good about yourself, you must be able to receive feelings. You are so good at caring for others, how about caring for yourself? You know how, but will you?

If you don't care for yourself, why not? Are you missing the motivation to change? If you want healthy and loving relationships, are you prepared to receive love when it is offered? Can you accept a relationship with a healthy person? Joy, love, beauty, compassion and peace are gifts to be received. Let them in. Obviously I hope you find your keys to recovery, but more importantly, find your locks. Use your keys and open them. Welcome the new life inside of you. Embrace it as an old friend. Welcome it home. Shout, "Let me take care of you as only I know how. Let me take care of me." In order to grow you will let much out, but your true growth will be measured by what you let in.

We have come far on this part of our journey. I have shared with you as far as we can go. My part of the journey is ending. Is yours beginning? I do not feel as if I am only the writer of this book. No writing experience of mine has ever created so many emotions in me. I have been more like a painter trying to capture a picture on canvas. I hope that my vision has been clear and that I have listened well on this journey. I now pass the map on to you. Now you will make the journey. Do not forget where you have been. As painful as it was, some of it will help as you travel. Learn to use those parts. Some things will weigh you down. Let those go. You have your choices and your map. Find your way. Find your love. Find your spirit. Find yourself.

Appendix

The Research Behind Perfect Daughters

Perfect Daughters is based on two related studies of adult daughters of alcoholic parents, conducted by the author. One study is of 125 adult daughters who offered written responses to open-ended questions about being a daughter of an alcoholic. The topics and quotations in the book are drawn from this "qualitative research." The other study is a quantitative analysis of the responses to a survey which was self-administered to two groups of women: 624 self-identified adult daughters and 585 women raised in non-alcoholic families. The statistics in the text are drawn largely from this study.

These two complementary studies provide comprehensive descriptions of the experiences of adult daughters of alcoholics. The quantitative data identifies the underlying characteristics of adult daughters, and the qualitative information shows the problem areas in which these characteristics are manifested or acted out. Most importantly, the two studies offer clarification and substantiation of the clinical observations plus personal anecdotes which have, heretofore, characterized the field.

The tables in this Appendix illustrate some of the findings of the two studies and complement the text of *Perfect Daughters*. If you would like further information about the study, please contact the author at Addiction Research and Consulting Services, 1705 Warren Road, Indiana, PA 15701.

Table 1. Background Differences Between ACoA Daughters and Non-ACoA Daughters

	ACoA n = 624	Non-ACoA n = 585
Background Information		
Minority	10%	10%
Married	77	74
Divorced	42	32*
Human Services Worker	84	89**
Drink Alcohol	61	71*
Perception Of Parents' Relationship*		
Poor	38%	11%
Below Average	30	18
Average	20	28
Above Average	11	41
Types Of Abuse In Family Of Origin		
Emotional Abuse	80%	37%*
Child Neglect	31	8*
Child Physical Abuse	31	9*
Child Sexual Abuse	19	5*
Spouse Abuse	38	6*
No Forms of Abuse	15	58*
Emotional Satisfaction Now*		
Very Low/Low	20%	10%
Moderate	45	38
High/Very High	34	51

*statistically significant at p__ .001
**statistically significant at p__ .05

Table 2. ACoA Daughters Compared to Non-ACoA Daughters on Dimensions and Items of the ACoA Index

	ACoA n = 624 mean (sd)	Non-ACoA n = 585 mean (sd)
Perceived Isolation	9.96 (2.4)	7.99 (2.0)
What is normal?	3.18 (.95)	2.52 (.85)
Feel different from others	3.25 (1.0)	2.73 (.87)
Difficulty with intimacy	3.53 (1.1)	2.74 (1.2)
Inconsistency	8.79 (2.4)	7.54 (1.9)
Difficulty following through	2.86 (1.1)	2.40 (.82)
Immediate gratification	3.06 (.97)	2.67 (.83)
Manage time poorly	2.87 (1.1)	2.47 (.92)
Self-Condemnation	10.72 (2.5)	8.77 (2.3)
Judge self without mercy	3.63 (1.1)	2.95 (1.0)
Difficulty having fun	3.16 (1.1)	2.44 (1.0)
Take self very seriously	3.92 (.90)	3.38 (.87)
Control Needs	6.84 (1.7)	5.54 (1.7)
Over-react to change	3.37 (.97)	2.82 (.87)
Super-responsible	3.46 (1.2)	2.72 (1.1)
Approval Needs	9.08 (2.1)	7.76 (1.8)
Seek approval and affirmation	3.51 (1.0)	3.00 (.91)
Loyal even when undeserved	3.39 (1.0)	2.98 (.98)
Lie when easy to tell truth	2.17 (.82)	1.78 (.69)
Rigidity	8.19 (2.3)	6.75 (2.0)
Lock self into a course	2.75 (.93)	2.27 (.79)
Seek tension and crisis	2.60 (1.0)	2.09 (.87)
Avoid conflict	2.84 (1.0)	2.34 (.92)
Fear Of Failure	9.58 (2.8)	7.73 (2.5)
Fear rejection and abandonment	3.03 (1.1)	2.30 (.97)
Fear criticism and judgment	3.14 (1.0)	2.64 (.94)
Fear failure	3.41 (1.1)	2.79 (1.2)
Total Score	62.13 (12.0)	52.52 (10.0)

All of the above are statistically significant at p__ .001

Scale: 5 = always, 4 = often, 3 = sometimes, 2 = seldom, 1 = never

Table 3. Problems Identified by
Adult Daughters of Alcoholics

	n = 125
	Percent

Unique Problems For ACoA Daughters Of Alcoholic Mothers

n = 47

Role model	45%
Relationships	36
Parenting skills	17
Identity	9
Trust	4
Other	13

Unique Problems For ACoA Daughters Of Alcoholic Fathers

n = 90

Relationships	40%
Role confusion	32
Intimacy	19
Sense of self	12
Sexual abuse	7
Perfectionism	4
Other	11

Most Significant Type Of Relationship Problems

n = 96

Trust	34%
Intimacy	28
Self-worth	27
Responsibility	23
Picking wrong partner	19
Other	21

Greatest Parenting Problems

n = 81

Need for control	33%
Don't know how to parent	19
Lack of consistency	16
Not able to meet child's needs	16
Other	20

Note: Percentages in each category equal more than 100 due to the fact that more than one problem was identified by some adult daughters.

Advice To Other ACoA Daughters

n = 66

Take care of yourself	30%
Get into a program	26
Use your past strengths	11
Know what you've missed	8
Associate with healthy people	6
Other	20

Note: Percentages in each category equal more than 100 due to the fact that more than one problem was identified by some adult daughters.

References

Ackerman, R. and Edward Gondolf. "Differentiating Adult Children of Alcoholics: The Effects of Background and Treatment on ACoA Symptoms." Paper presented at the American Sociological Association Annual Meeting, San Francisco, 1989.

Ackerman, R. "Adult Daughters of Alcoholics Study." Indiana University of Pennsylvania, Indiana, PA, 1988.

Ackerman, Robert J. **Abused No More: Recovery for Women from Abusive or Co-dependent Relationships.** HSI/TAB Books, Blue Ridge Summit, PA, 1989.

Ackerman, Robert J. **Same House, Different Homes: Why Adult Children Of Alcoholics Are Not All The Same.** Health Communications, Pompano Beach, FL, 1987.

Ackerman, Robert J. **Let Go And Grow: Recovery For Adult Children Of Alcoholics.** Health Communications, Pompano Beach, FL, 1987.

Bepko, Claudia. *The Responsibility Trap.* The Free Press, New York, 1985.

Berkowitz, Alan and H. Wesley Perkins. "Personality Characteristics of Children of Alcoholics." *Journal of Consulting and Clinical Psychology,* Vol. 56, No. 2, 206-209, 1988.

Blaker, Karen. **Born to Please.** St. Martin's Press, New York, 1988.

Cork, Margaret R. **The Forgotten Children.** Addiction Research Foundation, Toronto, Canada, 1969.

Cowan, Connell and Melvyn Kinder. **Smart Women, Foolish Choices.** Clarkson N. Potter, New York, 1985.

Erikson, Erik H. **Childhood and Society.** W. W. Norton, New York, 1963.

Garmezy, Norman et al as reported by Eleanor Hoover in *Human Behavior.* April, 1976.

"Having a Good Day" *USA Today,* April 13, 1989.

Hoff, Lee Ann. **People in Crisis,** 2nd ed., Addison-Wesley, Menlo Park, CA, 1984.

Hoopes, Margaret and James Harper. *Birth Order Roles and Sibling Patterns in Individual and Family Therapy.* Aspen Publishing, Rockville, MD, 1987.

Keri Report on Confidence and the American Woman, *USA Today,* 1988.

Maslow, Abraham H. **Toward a Psychology of Being.** Van Nostrand, New York, 1967.

Morehouse, Ellen and Tarpley Richards. "An Examination of Dysfunctional Latency Age Children of Alcoholic Parents and Problems in Intervention." *Journal of Children in Contemporary Society,* Vol. 15, #1, Fall 1982.

Niven, R. G. "Alcohol and the Family" in L. J. West ed. **Alcoholism and Related Problems.** Prentice-Hall, Englewood Cliffs, NJ, 1984.

Norwood, Robin. **Women Who Love Too Much.** Jeremy P. Tarcher, Los Angeles, 1985.

Obuchowska, I. "Emotional Contact with the Mother as a Social Compensatory Factor in Children of Alcoholics." *International Mental Health Research Newsletter,* 16(4), 2:4, 1974.

Perrin, Thomas W. "I Am An Adult Child of An Alcoholic." Thomas W. Perrin, 1984.

Sanford, Linda Tschirhart. "Women And Self-Esteem." Lecture given at Indiana University of Pennsylvania, Indiana, PA, April, 1988.

Sanford, Linda Tschirhart and Mary Ellen Donovan. **Women And Self-Esteem.** Anchor Press/Doubleday, New York, 1984.

Sexias, Judy and Geraldine Youcha. **Children of Alcoholism.** Crown Publishing, New York, 1985.

Sheehy, Gail. **Passages: Predictable Crises of Adult Life.** E. P. Dutton, New York, 1976.

Subby, Robert. **Lost In The Shuffle.** Health Communications, Pompano Beach, FL, 1987.

Volchok, Susan. "Childhood Labels." *Glamour,* July, 1985.

Werner, Emma. "Resilient Offspring of Alcoholics: A Longitudinal Study from Birth to Age 18." *Journal of Studies on Alcohol,* 47(1) 34-40, 1986.

Williams, Carol N. "Differences in Child Care Practices Among Families with Alcoholic Fathers, Alcoholic Mothers, and Two Alcoholic Parents." *Dissertation Abstracts International,* 44(01), 299-A, 1983.

Wilsnack, R. W.; Wilsnack, S.C. and A.D. Klassen. "Women's Drinking and Drinking Problems: Patterns from a 1981 National Survey." Paper presented at the Annual Meeting of the Society for the Study of Social Problems, San Francisco, September 1982.

Woititz, Janet G. **Adult Children of Alcoholics.** Health Communications, Pompano Beach, FL, 1983.

Zelditch, Morris. "Role Differentiation in the Nuclear Family: A Comparative Study" in Talcott Parsons and R. Bales eds. **Family, Socialization and Interaction Process.** Free Press, Glencoe, IL, 1955.

Other Books By Robert J. Ackerman

LET GO AND GROW
Recovery for Adult Children of Alcoholics

The book describes the characteristics of all adult children of alcoholics, plus the varying and diverse types. The author identifies the positive characteristics and pinpoints the problem areas.

ISBN 0-932194-51-6 (Soft cover 5½x8½ 196 pg.)
Code 4516 .... $8.95

GROWING IN THE SHADOW
Children of Alcoholics

Never before have the 21 leading national authorities on children of alcoholics been so effectively brought together as in this book which brings together the incisive objectivity of the leading experts in the field.

ISBN 0-932194-32-X (Soft cover 6x9 254 pg.)
Code 432X $9.95

SAME HOUSE DIFFERENT HOMES

Dr. Ackerman conducted a study of more than one thousand adults which produced positive solutions for adult children of alcoholics who grew up in dysfunctional homes.

ISBN 0-932194-43-5 (Soft cover 5½x8½ 70 pg.)
Code 4435 .... $3.95

CHILDREN OF ALCOHOLICS
A Bibliography and Resource Guide

This is the third edition of the complete bibliography on children of alcoholics, both adults and minors.

ISBN 0-932194-48-6 (Soft cover 5½x8½ 82 pg.)
Code 4486 .... $4.95

Enterprise Center, 3201 S.W. 15th Street,
Deerfield Beach, FL 33442
1-800-851-9100

Health Communications, Inc.

Other Books By . . .
Health Communications

ADULT CHILDREN OF ALCOHOLICS
Janet Woititz
Over a year on *The New York Times* Best-Seller list, this book is the primer on Adult Children of Alcoholics.
ISBN 0-932194-15-X $6.95

STRUGGLE FOR INTIMACY
Janet Woititz
Another best-seller, this book gives insightful advice on learning to love more fully.
ISBN 0-932194-25-7 $6.95

DAILY AFFIRMATIONS: For Adult Children of Alcoholics
Rokelle Lerner
These positive affirmations for every day of the year paint a mental picture of your life as you choose it to be.
ISBN 0-932194-27-3 $6.95

CHOICEMAKING: For Co-dependents, Adult Children and Spirituality Seekers — Sharon Wegscheider-Cruse
This useful book defines the problems and solves them in a positive way.
ISBN 0-932194-26-5 $9.95

LEARNING TO LOVE YOURSELF: Finding Your Self-Worth
Sharon Wegscheider-Cruse
"Self-worth is a choice, not a birthright," says the author as she shows us how we can choose positive self-esteem.
ISBN 0-932194-39-7 $7.95

BRADSHAW ON: THE FAMILY: A Revolutionary Way of Self-Discovery
John Bradshaw
The host of the nationally televised series of the same name shows us how families can be healed and individuals can realize full potential.
ISBN 0-932194-54-0 $9.95

HEALING THE CHILD WITHIN:
Discovery and Recovery for Adult Children of Dysfunctional Families
Charles Whitfield
Dr. Whitfield defines, describes and discovers how we can reach our Child Within to heal and nurture our woundedness.
ISBN 0-932194-40-0 $8.95

Enterprise Center, 3201 S.W. 15th Street,
Deerfield Beach, FL 33442
1-800-851-9100

Health
Communications, Inc.

New Books . . .
from Health Communications

HEALING THE SHAME THAT BINDS YOU
John Bradshaw
Toxic shame is the core problem in our compulsions, co-dependencies and addictions. The author offers healing techniques to help release the shame that binds us.
ISBN 0-932194-86-9 $9.95

THE MIRACLE OF RECOVERY:
Healing For Addicts, Adult Children and Co-dependents
Sharon Wegscheider-Cruse
Beginning with recognizing oneself as a survivor, it is possible to move through risk and change to personal transformation.
ISBN 1-55874-024-4 $9.95

CHILDREN OF TRAUMA: Rediscovering Your Discarded Self
Jane Middelton-Moz
This beautiful book shows how to discover the source of past traumas and grieve them to grow into whole and complete adults.
ISBN 1-55874-014-7 $9.95

New Books on Spiritual Recovery . . .

LEARNING TO LIVE IN THE NOW: 6-Week Personal Plan To Recovery
Ruth Fishel
The author gently introduces you step by step to the valuable healing tools of meditation, positive creative visualization and affirmations.
ISBN 0-932194-62-1 $7.95

CYCLES OF POWER: A User's Guide To The Seven Seasons of Life
Pamela Levin
This innovative book unveils the process of life as a cyclic pattern, providing strategies to use the seven seasons to regain power over your life.
ISBN 0-932194-75-3 $9.95

MESSAGES FROM ANNA: Lessons in Living (Santa Claus, God and Love)
Zoe Rankin
This is a quest for the meaning of "love." In a small Texas Gulf Coast town a wise 90-year-old woman named Anna shares her life messages.
ISBN 1-55874-013-9 $7.95

THE FLYING BOY: Healing The Wounded Man
John Lee
A man's journey to find his "true masculinity" and his way out of co-dependent and addictive relationships, this book is about feelings — losing them, finding them, expressing them.
ISBN 1-55874-006-6 $7.95

Enterprise Center, 3201 S.W. 15th Street,
Deerfield Beach, FL 33442
1-800-851-9100

Health
Communications, Inc.

Daily Affirmation Books from . . .
Health Communications

GENTLE REMINDERS FOR CO-DEPENDENTS: Daily Affirmations
Mitzi Chandler
With insight and humor, Mitzi Chandler takes the co-dependent and the adult child through the year. Gentle Reminders is for those in recovery who seek to enjoy the miracle each day brings.
ISBN 1-55874-020-1 $6.95

TIME FOR JOY: Daily Affirmations
Ruth Fishel
With quotations, thoughts and healing energizing affirmations these daily messages address the fears and imperfections of being human, guiding us through self-acceptance to a tangible peace and the place within where there is *time for joy.*
ISBN 0-932194-82-6 $6.95

CRY HOPE: Positive Affirmations For Healthy Living
Jan Veltman
This book gives positive daily affirmations for seekers and those in recovery. Every day is a new adventure, and change is a challenge.
ISBN 0-932194-74-5 $6.95

SAY YES TO LIFE: Daily Affirmations For Recovery
Father Leo Booth
These meditations take you through the year day by day with Father Leo Booth, looking for answers and sometimes discovering that there are none. Father Leo tells us, "For the recovering compulsive person God is too important to miss — may you find Him now."
IBN 0-932194-46-X $6.95

DAILY AFFIRMATIONS: For Adult Children of Alcoholics
Rokelle Lerner
Affirmations are a way to discover personal awareness, growth and spiritual potential, and self-regard. Reading this book gives us an opportunity to nurture ourselves, learn who we are and what we want to become.
ISBN 0-932194-47-3
(Little Red Book) $6.95
(New Cover Edition) $6.95

Enterprise Center, 3201 S.W. 15th Street,
Deerfield Beach, FL 33442
1-800-851-9100

Health
Communications, Inc.

Helpful 12-Step Books from . . .
Health Communications

HEALING A BROKEN HEART:
12 Steps of Recovery for Adult Children
Kathleen W.

This useful 12-Step book is presently the number one resource for all Adult Children support groups.

ISBN 0-932194-65-6   **$7.95**

12 STEPS TO SELF-PARENTING For Adult Children
Philip Oliver-Diaz and Patricia A. O'Gorman

This gentle 12-Step guide takes the reader from pain to healing and self-parenting, from anger to forgiveness, and from fear and despair to recovery.

ISBN 0-932194-68-0   **$7.95**

THE 12-STEP STORY BOOKLETS
Mary M. McKee

Each beautifully illustrated booklet deals with a step, using a story from nature in parable form. The 12 booklets (one for each step) lead us to a better understanding of ourselves and our recovery.

ISBN 1-55874-002-3   **$8.95**

WITH GENTLENESS, HUMOR AND LOVE:
A 12-Step Guide for Adult Children in Recovery
Kathleen W. and Jewell E.

Focusing on adult child issues such as reparenting the inner child, self-esteem, intimacy and feelings, this well-organized workbook teaches techniques and tools for the 12-step recovery programs.

ISBN 0-932194-77-X   **$7.95**

GIFTS FOR PERSONAL GROWTH & RECOVERY
Wayne Kritsberg

A goldmine of positive techniques for recovery (affirmations, journal writing, visualizations, guided meditations, etc.), this book is indispensable for those seeking personal growth.

ISBN 0-932194-60-5   **$6.95**

Enterprise Center, 3201 S.W. 15th Street,
Deerfield Beach, FL 33442
1-800-851-9100

Health Communications, Inc.

SUBSCRIBE TO THE MAGAZINE DEVOTED TO ADULT CHILDREN